ELVIS!

# ELVIS!

*An Illustrated Guide*

*to New and Vintage Collectibles*

S T E V E   T E M P L E T O N

COURAGE
BOOKS
AN IMPRINT OF RUNNING PRESS
PHILADELPHIA • LONDON

A QUINTET BOOK

9 8 7 6 5 4 3 2 1
Digit on the right indicates the number of this
printing.

Library of Congress Cataloging-in-Publication
Number 95-70141

ISBN 1-56138-711-8

This book was designed and produced by
Quintet Publishing Limited
6 Blundell Street
London N7 9BH

CREATIVE DIRECTOR: *Richard Dewing*
DESIGNER: *Simon Balley*
PROJECT EDITOR: *Stefanie Foster*
TEXT EDITOR: *Lydia Darbyshire*
PHOTOGRAPHER: *Colin Bowling*

*Quintet Publishing would like to extend very special
thanks to John Dieeso and Ted Young for so generously
opening up their homes and collections for photography,
and for their assistance on this book.*

Typeset in Great Britain by
Central Southern Typesetters, Eastbourne
Manufactured by Bright Arts (Singapore) Pte Ltd
Printed by Leefung Asco Printers Ltd, China

Published by Courage Books
an imprint of Running Press Book Publishers
125 South Twenty-second Street
Philadelphia, Pennsylvania 19103–4399

# C O N T E N T S

In 1956 Dwight D. Eisenhower was President of the United States, the New York Yankees won the World Series, Prince Rainier of Monaco married Grace Kelly, Floyd Patterson became the youngest boxer in history to win the world heavyweight championship – and the world of entertainment was about to be changed forever by the emergence of a young man who was to become the most popular entertainer the world had ever known. He ultimately was known only by his first name – Elvis.

Elvis Presley's impact went far beyond the music world, for it had a profound influence on American culture as well. When his first hit record "Heartbreak Hotel" reached the Number 1 slot in the spring of 1956, it was the first time that a record had achieved top position in the charts of all three of the main music papers, *Popular Music, Rhythm & Blues,* and *Country and Western*. In 1956 alone, Elvis had five No. 1 singles, and so great was the popularity of his records that RCA was forced to use the manufacturing facilities of other record companies to meet the demand.

It was not just the record industry that flourished with Elvis's enormous success, however. The singer's fame was quickly transformed into the first "celebrity bonanza" through the establishment of Elvis Presley Enterprises Incorporated. What followed was an avalanche of Elvis merchandise that left teenagers mesmerized by the appearance of Elvis's name and likeness on every imaginable item. Everything from clothes, costume jewelry, and suitcases, to board games, dolls, games, and much, much more were available to his growing legion of fans. This marketing venture was so successful that it has been estimated that by the end of 1956 merchandise licensed by Elvis Presley Enterprises grossed between $20 and $25 million. In the almost forty years since his first No. 1, Elvis's popularity has remained undimmed, and an ever-growing army of fans and collectors now seek the scarce and potentially valuable icons of the past. This is the world of Elvis memorabilia.

Price guides are given wherever possible. Collectors should note that these were rising even as the book was being written, but they provide a useful indication of how much Elvis memorabilia has increased in value.

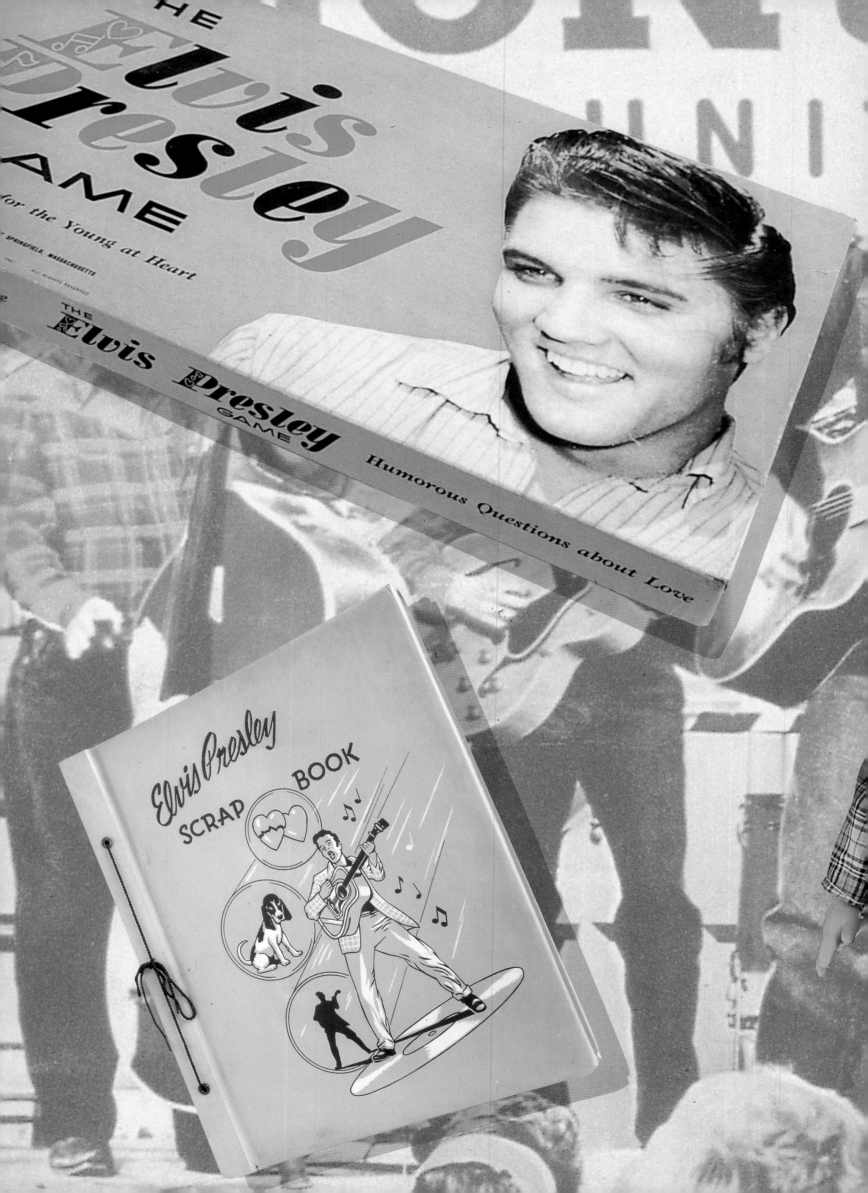

# BEGINNING
# TO
# COLLECT

To collect Elvis Presley memorabilia is to collect true Americana.

The facts testify to the almost unbelievable popularity of the singer. Over 1 billion Elvis records have been sold (enough to circle the globe twice if laid side by side); he appeared in 33 movies, each of which were a box-office success; in 1973, via worldwide satellite links, a concert he gave in Hawaii reached a television audience estimated at 1 billion. Although almost twenty years have passed since Elvis's death, hundreds of thousands of fans from all around the world travel each year to Memphis, Tennessee, to visit Graceland and to pay homage to the legend who not only made an indelible mark on American history, but also influenced the entire world.

Much of the enjoyment derived from collecting Elvis memorabilia is the wide range of items that are available. Apart from the items directly related to the music – the records and sheet music – there are novelty items, postcards, RCA memorabilia, pictures, and film-related articles. Since 1977, a new range of merchandise has flooded onto the market, and collectors are adding some of these newer items, such as decanters, trading cards and dolls, to their collections.

Added to the excitement of collecting the memorabilia is the pleasure to be derived from visiting Graceland, the second most often visited home in the U.S.A. Since 1982, when it was first opened to the public, fans and admirers from around the world have poured in. In recent years, their numbers have risen from 40,000 a year to an estimated 700,000 in 1994. Graceland offers the visitor the opportunity to see Elvis's house and to pay tribute to the man, his music, and his movies. Aircraft, including the *Lisa Marie*, owned and used by Elvis both for concert tours and general travel can be seen there, and there is a museum and small theater. There are also gift shops carrying an array of Elvis memorabilia.

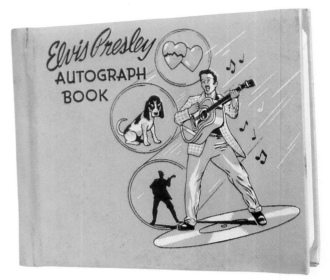

ABOVE: **Autograph Book**
**$450–550**

These five items all feature the same likeness, and they are often referred to as the "pink items" by collectors. The record case, diary, and autograph book are the hardest to find of the five items. An even rarer five-year diary does exist. All items carry the Elvis Presley Enterprises 1956 trade mark.

ABOVE: **Photograph Album**
**$400–500**

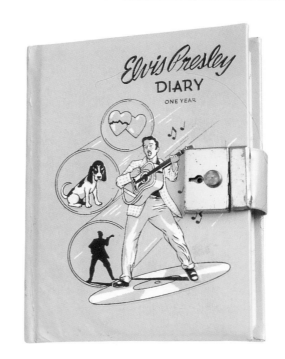

ABOVE: **Diary**
$450–600

ABOVE: **Scrap Book**
$400–500

RIGHT: **Record Case**
$450–600

## VALUE

As with all fields of collecting, many people look at Elvis collectibles with a view to investment. It is true that many of the rarer articles, especially the novelty items that appeared in 1956 and 1957, have greatly increased in value over the last 15 years. A board game that retailed for $3.98 when it first appeared in 1957, for example, was sold in 1984 for $400. If that same game were to appear on the market today it would probably sell for about $1,000. However, no one should begin to collect memorabilia simply with the idea of making money. Acquire items that appeal to you – that you find attractive or pleasing because of their associations. Enjoy owning them for their own sake. If they gain in value over the years, it's a bonus.

The value of Elvis memorabilia is generally determined by the same criteria that govern the value of other collectibles – condition, scarcity, and demand. Other factors, such as detailing, craftsmanship, and age, can also affect value.

ABOVE: **The bubble gum display box, which bears the Elvis Presley Enterprises 1956 mark, is very attractive and highly sought by collectors. The bubble gum wrappers are** both considered rare. The 5¢ **wrapper, which features a picture of Elvis, is more in demand.**
**Display box: $700–900**
**1¢ wrapper: $75–100**
**5¢ wrapper: $150–200**

RIGHT AND BELOW: **The 1957 board game is one of the most attractive of the Elvis Presley Enterprises items. The game originally sold for $3.98 and was manufactured by Teen-Age Games Inc., West Springfield, Massachusetts. $1,200–1,500**

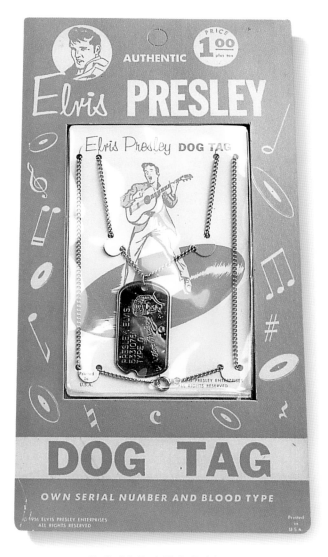

## CONDITION

The condition of an object will determine whether it is worth its full potential value. An article in mint condition must be clean and free from all marks, tears, and discoloration. An item that has been subject to considerable wear would be worth less than the same object in pristine condition.

Another important factor is the original packaging, which can add considerably to the value of any article. This is especially true when it comes to the jewelry that appeared in the 1950s. Most items of jewelry were presented on cards to hold them in place and to display them. The cards themselves were often attractively illustrated and produced, and in addition, they carried information about the maker and about

the copyright. A piece of jewelry that is still attached to its original card will carry a considerable premium compared to a similar piece without the card.

Some kinds of merchandise were sold in attractive outer packaging, and the existence of the original box or packaging can really enhance the value of the article. The dog-tag necklace is a prime example. The necklace itself is rather common by collectors' standards, but when it is found with its complete packaging, this piece becomes rare and keenly sought

BELOW: **The 1956 EPE earrings had a 14 karat gold-plated finish and were made to match the Elvis charm bracelet. If the earrings are still on their original card, their value is increased** considerably. The card was black with gold lettering and bore the 1956 EPE copyright. The line of jewelry also included a very rare guitar pin.
**Earrings only: $150–200**
**Earrings on card: $400–500**

**Shortly after Elvis's induction into the army in March 1958, Elvis Presley Enterprises issued a line of dog-tag jewelry bearing Elvis's army number, 55310761. All the items were attached to cards that have the 1956 Elvis Presley Enterprise copyright. A woman's version of the dog-tag bracelet was also available. A dog-tag anklet, sweater guard, and key chain were also produced. The EPE dog-tag necklace as illustrated still on its packaging is very rare. In 1977 Factors Inc. reproduced the necklace, but it was manufactured with a gold finish rather than the original chrome.**

after. This is, of course, because when the necklace was originally bought, the card and packaging were almost always discarded as soon as the purchaser got the necklace home. The packaging is truly scarce and adds immeasurably to the value.

A similar situation arises with the early 45 RPM records. Today the original covers are, in many cases, more keenly collected than the records themselves. The boxes in which the shoes were packaged are so rare that they, too, command a high premium.

The value is also, of course, affected by rarity of the piece itself. Clearly, if there are a large number of a product available, the item's value will remain relatively steady. Nevertheless, scarcity alone will not drive up the value of an article. If there is little or no demand for something, no matter how rare it is, the price will remains constant. A good example are the 24-sheet billboard-size movie posters, which are very scarce. However, given their huge size and their original purpose, the average collector has little interest in them. The one-sheet or three-sheet posters, on the other hand, increase in value and demand because collectors can display them easily and enjoy them as decorative objects.

ABOVE: **The 1956 EPE charm bracelet on the blue card is the Canadian version. The U.S. version was attached to a white card with red printing. The bracelets are otherwise identical.
Canadian version (blue card): $125–150
U.S. version (white card): $200–225**

## DEMAND

The other factor that affects value is demand. Individual collectors who want a single item to complete a set will often pay more than a general collector. Dealers who specialize in this area may also seek to buy up items so that they can attract customers, or they may be asked to look out for particular articles. When the new trading cards were introduced, both dealers and fans were eager to buy the handsomely produced cards. Time alone will tell if they have the potential to become true Elvis collectibles.

Sometimes rarity and demand coincide. A perfect example is the Paint-by-Number Set that appeared in 1957. This beautiful item originally sold for less than $2.00. Today, this article, in good condition, could

BELOW: **"Mr. Rhythm"** is the first known souvenir program with Elvis on the cover. This eight-page booklet was sold during the early part of 1956, and Elvis is featured on three of the pages, with the other stars performing at this time appearing on the other pages. A photograph of Elvis is also included on the back cover.
**$300–400**

BELOW: **"Mr. Dynamite"** is the first souvenir program devoted exclusively to Elvis. On the first printing, the word "album" was spelled "albun," an error corrected on later versions. The program was originally sold during the summer of 1956.
**$275–300**

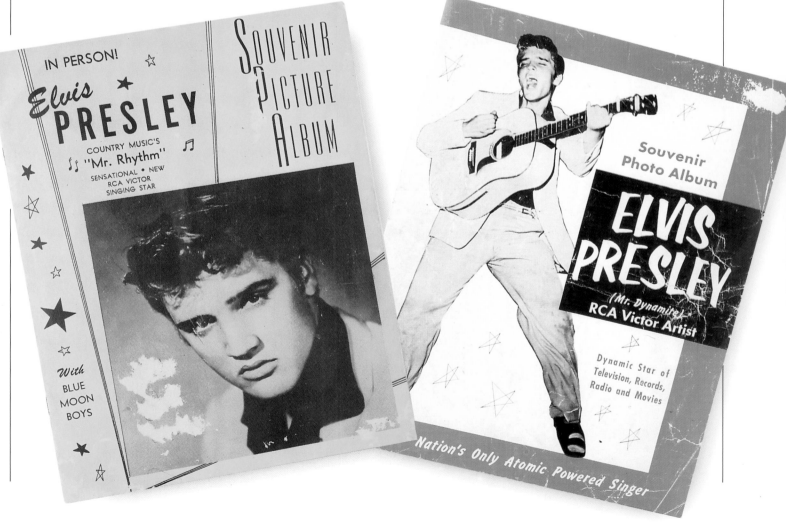

easily fetch more than $1,000 – it is therefore one of the rarest but also most desirable of all Elvis collectibles.

Newcomers to collecting Elvis memorabilia should be aware that items dating from the 1950s and 1960s are already well established as collectors' items. Few people who bought these articles when they first appeared had the foresight to know that thirty or forty years later they would be regarded as collectible and desirable objects. This is not to say that items made recently should not be appreciated, and since Elvis Presley Enterprises regained control of licensed merchandising, the quality of the memorabilia available has improved enormously. However, whether they will be as keenly collected in thirty or forty years' time as the objects produced in the 1950s and 1960s is impossible to say. The guiding rule for any collector must be to acquire items that he or she likes and wants to own. Have fun and enjoy the hunt, and do

ABOVE: **Movie preview programs, which were particularly popular with advertisers at drive-in movies.
Each program: $7–10**

not let thoughts of future value prevent you from adding pieces to your collection.

This rule – that collecting Elvis memorabilia should be fun – is especially applicable to someone who is just beginning to build up a collection. Whether you pay a lot or very little for an item, you should be buying because it is something you want. Do not buy to speculate on future value. If something does appreciate in value, you will have that pleasure to add to your enjoyment in owning it; if it fails to gain in value or even falls in value, you will not be disappointed.

An example of this would be if the opportunity to acquire the Elvis Presley Enterprises (EPE) 1957 doll. This is the only doll to be manufactured that was authorized by EPE during the singer's lifetime. In addition, it is considered one of the rarest of all Elvis collectibles. Examples of the doll in excellent or near mint condition are generally in great demand among long-time collectors. The doll's value will be enhanced if it is wearing the original clothes. Other points of interest, further increasing its value for collectors, are the orange sticker with the inscription "Elvis Presley" attached to the belt and, of course, the original box. If you were to be offered a doll in this condition, what should you do? Your response will depend on the kind of collector you are and on your reasons for considering this expensive acquisition.

If you are a long-established collector and you are especially interested in the novelty items produced in the 1950s, especially the 1956 and 1957 Elvis Presley

RIGHT: **This is the only doll manufactured by Elvis Presley Enterprises during the singer's lifetime, and it is one of the rarest Elvis collectibles ever. It originally sold for $3.98, stands 16 inches high, and was sold dressed in a plaid shirt, blue trousers, blue suede shoes, and a black belt. The belt originally had Elvis's name printed on it.**
**Doll only with complete clothing: $1,500–1,800**
**Doll with clothing and box: $1,900–2,400**

Enterprises items, the doll will be of great interest. Someone who is just beginning to build up a collection or someone who is interested in other areas of memorabilia may want to think very carefully before committing themselves to such a major purchase, however. You may, for example, feel that the novelty items of the 1950s are over-priced. You might also bear in mind that many collectors do not particularly like this doll because it is such a poor representation of Elvis. In addition, the doll's body is made of lightweight rubber, and this has caused it to deteriorate over the years if it was not properly cared for and exposed to the elements. Further, the doll is keenly sought only by collectors of Elvis memorabilia and not by doll collectors in general, which will limit its appeal somewhat.

Finally, of course, you should consider your own financial status. Only buy within your means. A good collector is a smart buyer, not an emotional buyer. Emotional or obsessive collecting can ultimately destroy your love of collecting and even place you in serious financial difficulties. Remember: a collectible is only worth what you are willing to pay for it.

Before we look at some of the more desirable and collectible items of Elvis memorabilia, let me offer a word of warning about merchandise that bears what might be termed "intensified labeling" – that is,

BELOW: **The 1956 RCA personal appearance contract. Approximately 3 feet in length, this contract, which was drawn up by Colonel Parker for Elvis's 1956 appearance, is without doubt one of the most legendary pieces of memorabilia, worth over $1,500.**

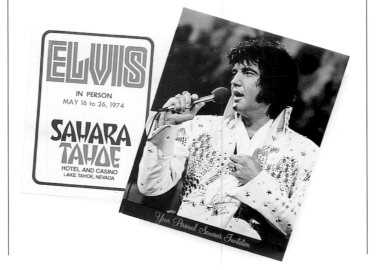

RIGHT: **A Tahoe invitation menu – personal VIP invitation. This illustration clearly shows the outer envelope that contained the invitations and menu for one of Elvis's Tahoe shows.**

BELOW: **The RIAA (Record Industry Association of America) Gold Sales Award.** In addition to the recording artist, a gold record award is presented to those people directly responsible for the record and its success. Very few awards were handed out – estimates of 12 to 20. Reads: "Presented to Buck Davis to commemorate the sale of more than 500,000 copies of the long-playing record album *Moody Blue*."

ABOVE: **This concert scarf was originally obtained by a fan, given directly to her by Elvis while attending a concert in Steveport, Louisiana, in the 1970s. The** note accompanying the scarf is written and signed by Priscilla Presley. The letter was directed to the wife of one of Elvis's head security men.

products marked "limited edition" or "collector's series." In many instances, these labels are nothing more than an easy means of enhancing the article to which they are attached. A good product that is intrinsically attractive and appealing needs no such gimmick to entice buyers.

For this reason, items that were created during the 1950s and those that were produced throughout Elvis's career are the true icons of the past and merit being collected as such. When the first merchandise appeared in 1956, no one thought of collecting the articles as potential investments. People bought products because they liked them, and they used them for the purposes for which they were intended, often discarding them when they had outlived their use,

thus, inadvertently, creating the shortages that have produced the expensive collectibles of today.

It is only natural for collectors to enjoy possessing and acquiring articles that appreciate in value. However, it should never be forgotten that newly marketed products that appear to be skyrocketing in value through the activities of over-zealous dealers are nothing more than traps for the unwary buyer.

Always remember that acquiring items is one of the ways in which a collector can "romanticize the past," and a good product will appeal to any collector's yesterday. Buy only what really appeals to you and be true to your own sense of the past. Put aside all thoughts of collecting for investment purposes – and have fun.

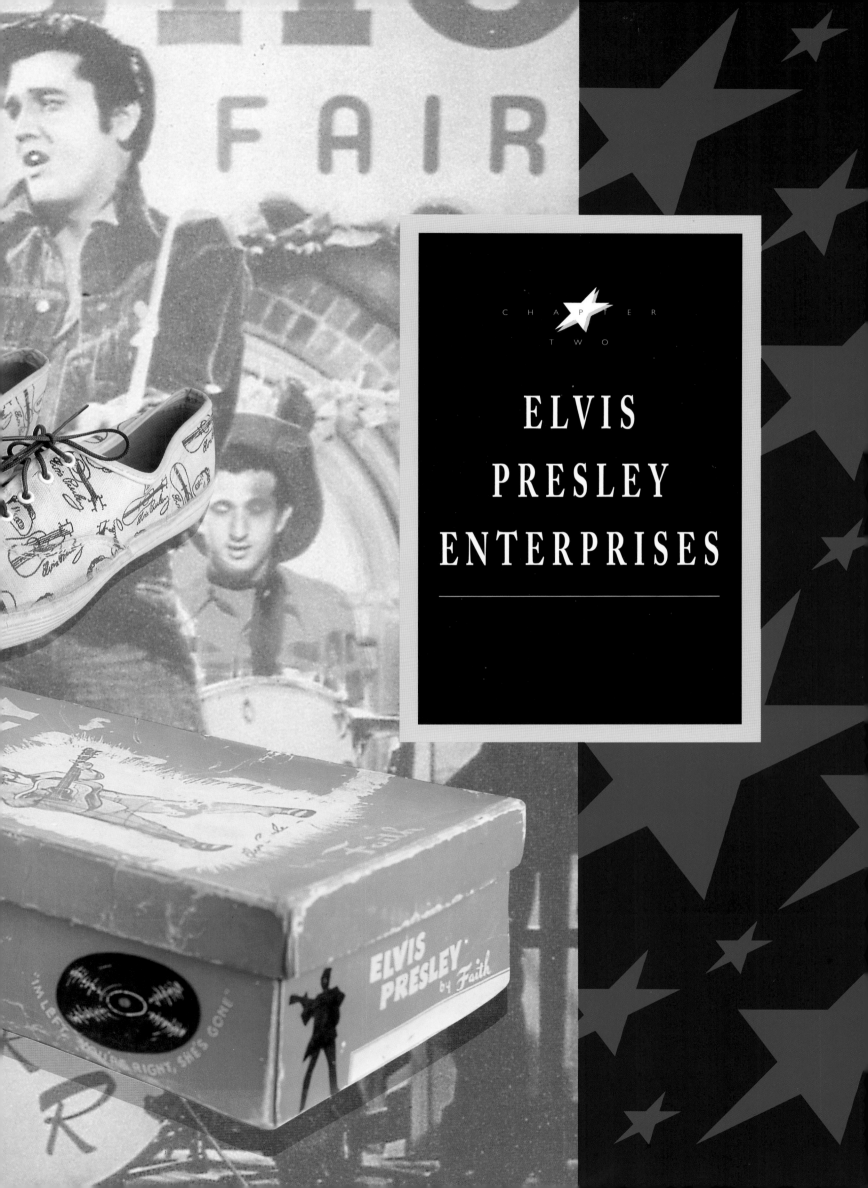

CHAPTER TWO

# ELVIS PRESLEY ENTERPRISES

Almost anyone who enjoys watching television or old films will be quite familiar with the teams of Laurel and Hardy, Abbott and Costello, or Burns and Allen. These are just a few of the most popular and successful partnerships in the history of show business, and their great success was due not only to the unique talents of each member of the team, but also to the ways in which each of the partners supported and built on the strengths of the other.

Among these legendary partnerships must be counted a unique duo which came together in August 1955. This team was the relatively unknown southern singer, Elvis Presley, and his newly acquired manager, Colonel Tom Parker. Although each member of this partnership had greatly contrasting talents, their

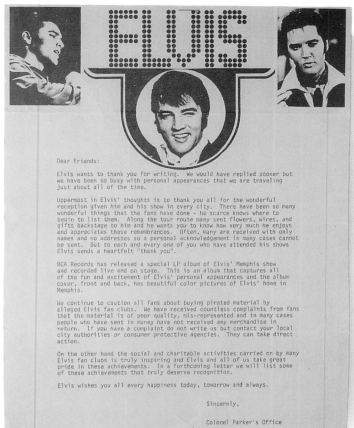

ABOVE: **A form letter from Colonel Parker's office.**

LEFT: **"Happy New Year" from the Colonel's office.**

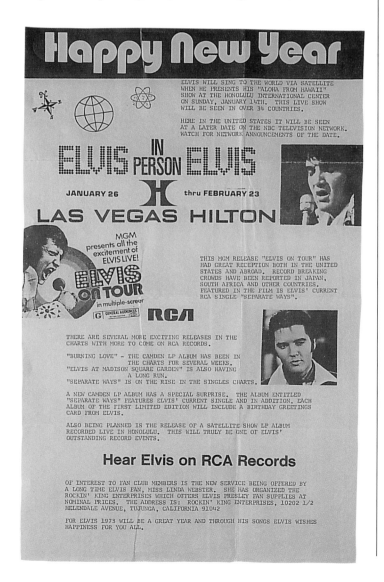

abilities combined perfectly, offering a unique musical talent with a shrewd show-business mind. Elvis would, of course, have been a success without the aid of Colonel Parker, but without the Colonel's shrewd promotional know-how and his knowledge of the music business, it is possible that the magnitude of that success would have been different.

From the early days of 1954, Elvis was transformed from a singer who was well known in a limited region of the United States to a celebrity known throughout the world, making him one of the most idolized and influential figures in the history of popular music. Through music, television, and film, Elvis reshaped the popular concept of culture. He soon came to be the real-life hero for hundreds of

LEFT AND BELOW: **The Elvis Presley bubble gum cards bear the Elvis Presley Enterprises 1956 mark. There were 66 cards to form a complete set. The set consisted of two separate series. Cards 1–46 represent the "Ask Elvis" series. On the back of these cards is a question and answer about Elvis. Cards 47–66 are scenes from Elvis's first movie,** *Love Me Tender.* **Set: $600–800**

thousands of adoring fans, and part of this achievement was the result of his collaboration with Colonel Parker.

In the spring of 1956, Elvis Presley was incorporated and copyrighted in the form of Elvis Presley Enterprises, a move made with the encouragement and under the direction of Colonel Parker. "Heartbreak Hotel" had just reached No. 1 when Parker recruited the services of the California businessman and promoter, Henry "Hank" Saperstein. Saperstein's previous experience included the promotion of merchandise associated with the TV programs *Wyatt Earp*, *The Lone Ranger*, *Lassie*, and

ABOVE AND BELOW: **These shoes, which originally sold for $4.99, were available in leather (as illustrated) or in fabric. They were manufactured by Faith Shoe Co. and were marked with Elvis Presley Enterprises 1956. The box that contained the shoes is very rare and carries a high premium.**
**Shoes (pair): $800–1,000**
**Box: $300–500**

RIGHT: **The felt skirt originally sold for $2.98. Similar skirts in corduroy and denim were also available. The skirt was manufactured by Little Jean Togs Inc. and bore the Elvis Presley Enterprises 1956 mark.** $1,000–1,200

BELOW: **The blue jeans tag, which is marked Elvis Presley Enterprises 1956, was attached to the black twill jeans with green stitching. The jeans originally sold for $2.98 and were manufactured by Blue Ridge Manufacturers. Tag only: $100–150**

*Davy Crockett.* One of his greatest successes had been with Davy Crockett's "coonskin hat." Parker wanted Saperstein to market Elvis merchandise in the same way.

Under the direction of Parker and the guidance of Saperstein, Elvis Presley Enterprises contracted and issued a limited number of licences to manufacturers for items that would carry Elvis's name and likeness. The initial contracts scheduled more than 180 items for manufacture and promotion.

The first of the products to be mass-marketed was the charm bracelet, and RCA had been given exclusive rights to distribute it. More than 350,000 were sold in just one month, and this was followed by a veritable avalanche of merchandise – everything from clothes to games and jewelry to suitcases. A teenager could be dressed from head to toe in Elvis merchandise and be doing homework with pens and pencils and notebooks bearing the singer's name and likeness or playing the new Elvis game with friends.

When sales figures became available, one New York clothing manufacturer was shown to have sold

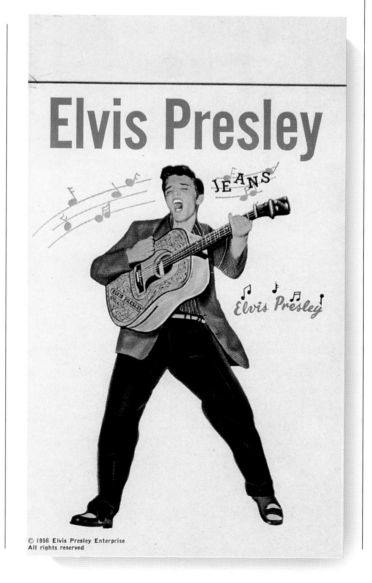

ABOVE AND LEFT: **The sneakers and sneakers box were manufactured by the Randolph Manufacturing Company and bore the mark Elvis Presley Enterprises 1956. Illustrated are the two different colors that were available in 1956. The box that contained the sneakers is extremely scarce.**
**Sneakers: $700–900**
**Box only: $400–500**

LEFT: **The T-shirt is also known as a crew-neck polo shirt. A boat-neck shirt and pajamas were also available. All the garments bore the Elvis Presley Enterprises 1956 mark. $350–450**

80,000 pairs of black twill jeans with green stitching, retailing at $12.98 a pair. Elvis lipstick passed the 45,000 mark at $1.00 each. Sales of the bronze statuette that had to be bought by mail order rather than purchased in a store exceeded 150,000. It was reported that 240,000 T-shirts were sold, together with 7,200 pairs of Elvis tennis shoes. So successful was this mass-marketing venture that it has been estimated that, by the end of 1956, Elvis Presley Enterprises had grossed between $20 and $25 million.

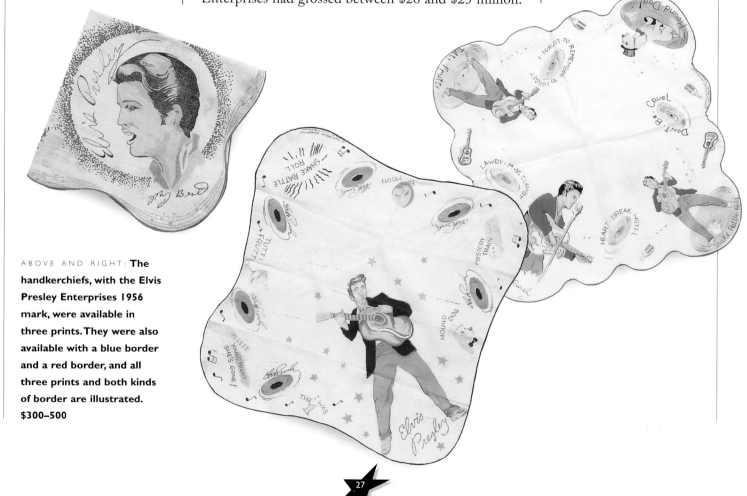

ABOVE AND RIGHT: **The handkerchiefs, with the Elvis Presley Enterprises 1956 mark, were available in three prints. They were also available with a blue border and a red border, and all three prints and both kinds of border are illustrated. $300–500**

LEFT: **The scarf was available in three different colors and sizes. The scarf that is illustrated is white and measures 32 x 32 inches. This delicate scarf features a four-color print on a blend of rayon and silk. Two smaller types of scarves – referred to as a kerchief and a turban – were also available. The scarf illustrated here, which has the Elvis Presley Enterprises 1956 mark, originally sold for $1.49. $400–600**

After the boom year of 1956, Elvis Presley Enterprises slowed down its marketing efforts. Elvis's own success meant that there was no longer any need to promote the merchandise so assiduously. By the end of 1956, Elvis had recorded five No. 1 singles and he had also made his first movie, *Love Me Tender*. He had become a major star.

The following year, 1957, proved to be as dramatic as 1956. On January 6, Elvis made his third and final appearance on the *Ed Sullivan Show*. This was the notorious "from the waist up" performance, because CBS censors would not allow the television cameras to show Elvis below the waist. Elvis had become such an impressive performer that Steven Allen suggested to NBC executives that his own show, which was screened opposite the *Ed Sullivan Show*, be replaced by a movie. Allen had played host to Elvis just a few months before, and he was well aware of the singer's popularity. (NBC did, in fact, show a movie.)

After the success he had enjoyed in the song charts between June and December 1956, Elvis continued into 1957 in the same vein with four more Number 1 hits. He also appeared as Deke Rivers in Paramount's *Loving You* and as the rebellious ex-convict Vince Everett in MGM's *Jailhouse Rock*.

ABOVE: **The mittens originally sold for $1.50 a pair. They were available in red, white, and navy, and they were manufactured by Nolon Gloves. They are marked Elvis Presley Enterprises 1956. Pair: $700–900**

Despite the critics who were scornful of his acting abilities, it was clear from box-office receipts that movie audiences were as enthralled with Elvis's presence as were the record buyers.

Although production was somewhat scaled down compared with 1956's output, Elvis Presley Enterprises were not totally silent during 1957. Of the few new products that were licensed in that year, three of the items are among the rarest and most keenly collected of all Elvis memorabilia. These are the paint by numbers set, the game, and the doll. Other items from this year that are in great demand among collectors are the "glow-in-the-dark picture" and the *Photo Folio Tour Book.*

BELOW: **The 1956 EPE pencil sharpener enabled fans to keep their homework assignments neat by keeping their Elvis Presley pencils well sharpened. $200–250**

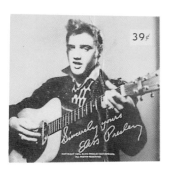

RIGHT: **EPE pencil and pre-price tag 1956 from 1956. As the pre-price tag illustrates, a pack of pencils originally cost 39¢. A pack consisted of 12 pencils in** four different colors, and each pencil bore the printed words "Sincerely yours, Elvis Presley." **Pencils in pack: $200–300 Pre-price tag: $25–50**

RIGHT: **The 1956 EPE bookend was made by Sanjan Co. It stands approximately 7 inches high and has a glossy ivory-colored finish. The approximate cost for a single bookend was $1.29. Single bookend: $300–450**

BELOW: **"Elvis Presley Souvenir Photo Album" contains 12 black and white photographs. Issued during the latter part of 1956, it carries the 1956 Elvis Presley Enterprises copyright line. $175–200**

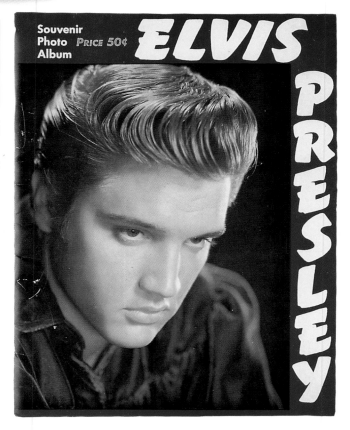

After 1957, with one or two exceptions, Elvis Presley Enterprises produced very little. The exceptions were a gold-plated bust of Elvis, which was made in 1961, and a silver-plated necklace and bracelet, issued to promote the 1962 movie, *Follow That Dream*. In fact, although the gold-plated bust carried the Elvis Presley Enterprises copyright, it was actually a promotional item from the record company RCA Victor. After 1962 Elvis Presley Enterprises was not involved with the manufacturing of any new merchandise until 1982.

Before Elvis's death, merchandise bearing the copyright of Boxcar Enterprises was produced during the period the singer was performing on tour. The contract with Boxcar was drawn up in 1974, and it is reported that Colonel Parker received the greater part

LEFT: **"Elvis Presley Photo Folio"** was the last souvenir program to be issued in the 1950s. The first impressions featured an advertisement for the movie *Jailhouse Rock* on the back cover, but subsequent printing featured an advertisement promoting Elvis's new album, "Elvis Golden Records." This program carries the 1957 Elvis Presley Enterprises copyright line. **$175–200**

ABOVE: **In 1977 Boxcar Enterprises made an agreement with Perth Pewter to manufacture three limited-edition pewter figurines representing three different aspects of Elvis's career: the early years, the** movies, and the Vegas years. **Each figure was approximately 5 inches high and was signed by the artist, Rose Spicer. Each figure originally sold for $50. $75–150**

BELOW: **An advertisement by Boxcar Enterprises for the three pewter figures under the promotional slogan: "The Legend Lives On."**

of the profits from the sale of merchandise, with Elvis himself earning 15 percent of the total sales.

Almost immediately after Elvis's death, Colonel Parker persuaded the singer's father, Vernon Presley, to join him in a partnership known as Factors Etc. Incorporated. Factors Etc. was a company that had been founded by Harry Geisler in Bear, Delaware, and at one time it had global rights to Elvis merchandise and was the largest merchandising company in the world. The contract with Parker and Vernon Presley related to all Elvis-related merchandise except the music and films. However, in July 1981 it was decided in court that Factors Inc. had no rights to merchandise the Presley name – so, re-enter Elvis Presley Enterprises.

LEFT: **An in-store display unit for Chu-Bops, made by Factors for Boxcar Enterprises in 1981. $20–30**

RIGHT: **This store counter display box for Chu-Bops holds mini-LPs. The "LPs," in fact, contain bubble gum. It was made by Factors for Boxcar Enterprises in 1981. $40–65**

# SUN AND
# RCA

## SUN

The start of the real life fairy tale began on a hot summer day in Memphis, Tennessee, in 1953. An 18-year-old named Elvis Presley walked into Memphis Recording Service, paid his $4.00, and recorded the song "My Happiness" coupled with "That's When Your Heartaches Begin." According to legend, Elvis recorded these songs with the intention of giving them to his mother, Gladys Presley, as a birthday present.

Legend further relates that Elvis shortly afterward received an invitation from Memphis Recording Service to return to the studio so that Sam Phillips, the producer of Sun Records, could listen more closely to what he thought might be an innovative voice and recording style. Late in 1954, after several

BELOW: **The "Louisiana Hayride" photograph. This 1955 black and white photograph is sometimes referred to as the "Tuxedo" picture. It measures 8 x 10 inches. The "Hayride" picture was one of the first souvenir photographs to be sold or given away of the young Elvis. This picture is extremely rare and is highly sought by collectors of 1950s Elvis memorabilia. $100–125**

BELOW: **This Elvis Sun promotional photograph is interesting for several reasons. First, it may be the first-ever Sun publicity photograph of Elvis. Second, not only does the photograph display an authentic Elvis autograph, but when the picture is turned over, the signatures of Scotty Moore and Bill Black are also inscribed. Talk about history! $400–700**

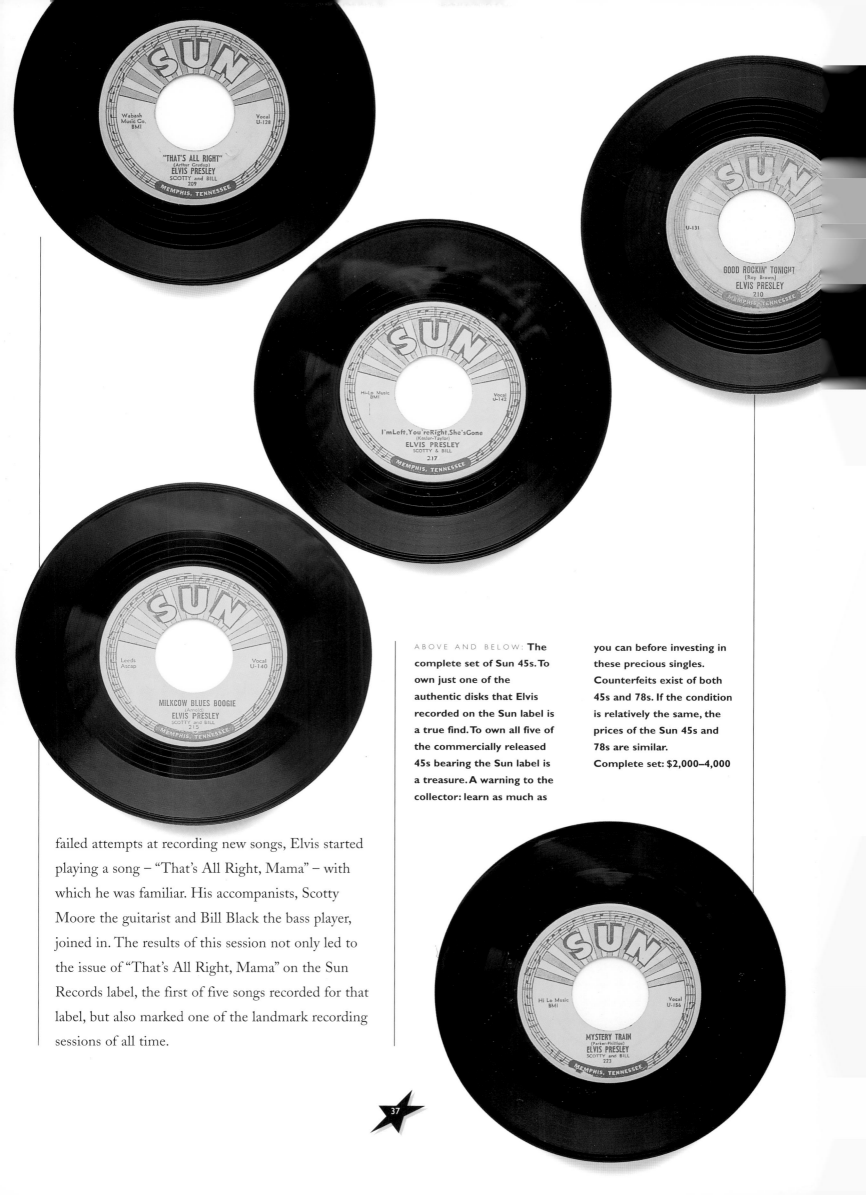

failed attempts at recording new songs, Elvis started playing a song – "That's All Right, Mama" – with which he was familiar. His accompanists, Scotty Moore the guitarist and Bill Black the bass player, joined in. The results of this session not only led to the issue of "That's All Right, Mama" on the Sun Records label, the first of five songs recorded for that label, but also marked one of the landmark recording sessions of all time.

On July 11, 1955, Elvis recorded what was to be his fifth and last disk at Sun Studio in Memphis, Tennessee. The recordings of "Mystery Train" and "I Forgot to Remember to Forget" ended a magical era, and now Elvis's recordings for Sun are regarded as the very best of his output. Not only do they represent the beginning of a remarkable music career, but for many they epitomize the entire hobby of collecting Elvis records and memorabilia.

Other records and items of merchandise may be valued more highly in strict monetary terms, but certainly from the historic point of view and their significance in Elvis's later career, they cannot be surpassed. But before you rush out to spend all your money, you should be aware of one or two problems.

As with so many highly regarded objects, counterfeits of the Sun records exist. If you are offered what purports to be a Sun recording, remember that the original labels are a deep yellow with dark brown printing; most counterfeit versions have lighter or softer yellow labels with light brown or black printing. The original records were not made on colored vinyl; they did not have "Issued 1973" engraved in the vinyl; and no original Sun recording has "RE" or "Reissue" engraved in the vinyl. In addition, no picture sleeves were issued with the Sun originals.

Authentic Sun records have either three indentations on the label, signifying a Memphis pressing, or a small triangle etched into the vinyl near the record label, signifying a California pressing. Suns were printed in both Memphis and California, and while purists may prefer the Memphis versions, the Suns that were printed in California may be rarer. Both pressings are original, however.

BELOW: **"That's All Right, Mama" (78)**

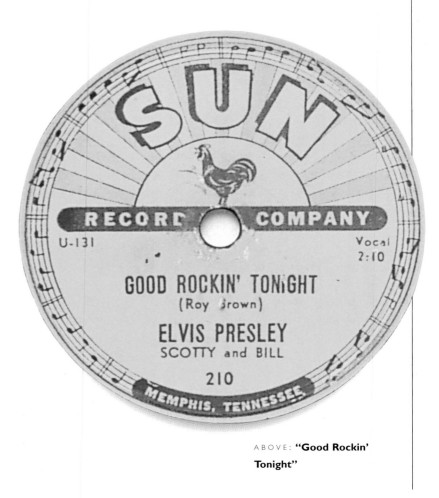

ABOVE: **"Good Rockin' Tonight"**

LEFT: **"Milk Cow Blues Boogie"**

## R C A

The sheer volume of advertising produced by RCA in connection with its promotion of Elvis's records is almost overwhelming, and there is far too much to be included in a book of this length. An entire volume would be needed to do justice to this one area of memorabilia, and so the remainder of this chapter looks at the main area that the novice collector is likely to encounter.

THIS PAGE AND OPPOSITE: **All five Sun records. What more could a collector want? Complete set: $2,000–4,000**

BELOW: **"I'm Left, You're Right, She's Gone"**

ABOVE: **"Mystery Train"**

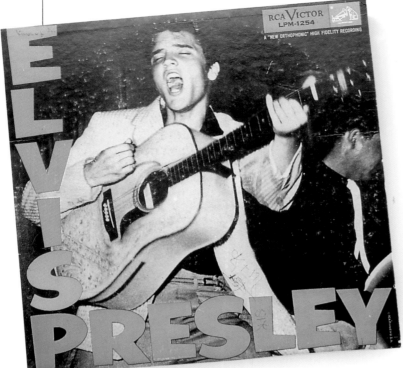

LEFT: **This is the first album (LPM-1254) Elvis recorded for RCA.**
**$75–125**

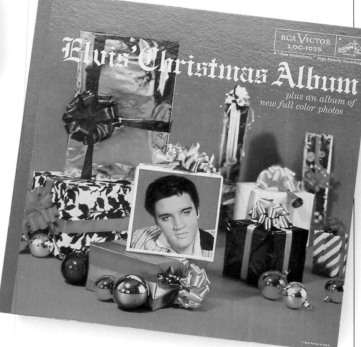

RIGHT AND BELOW:

**Although this album was re-released in 1985 by RCA, the original version, "Elvis Christmas Album" (LOC-1035), remains the most sought-after album by Elvis** that was ever released commercially by RCA. $150–300; if the little gold foil gift sticker is still attached to the album, add $100–150 to the value.

SIDE 1
SANTA CLAUS IS BACK IN TOWN
WHITE CHRISTMAS
HERE COMES SANTA CLAUS
(Right Down Santa Claus Lane)
I'LL BE HOME FOR CHRISTMAS
BLUE CHRISTMAS
SANTA BRING MY BABY BACK (To Me)
SIDE 2
OH LITTLE TOWN OF BETHLEHEM
SILENT NIGHT
(There'll Be) PEACE IN THE VALLEY (For Me)
I BELIEVE
TAKE MY HAND, PRECIOUS LORD
IT IS NO SECRET (What God Can Do)

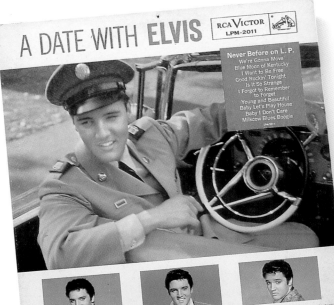

Another highly sought album is "A Date with Elvis" (LPM-2011). The reverse featured a 1960 calendar with the incorrect date of Elvis's discharge from the Army – March 24 is circled on the calendar, but the date Elvis was discharged was March 5, 1960. $100–150; an aluminum foil advertisement that was originally draped over the album can add considerably to the album's value.

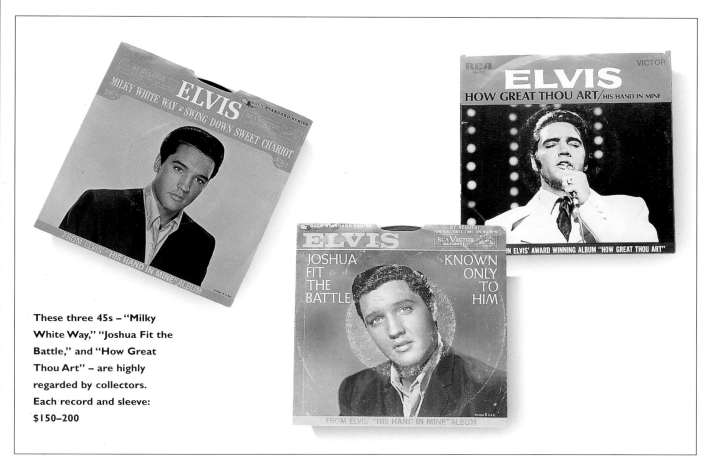

These three 45s – "Milky White Way," "Joshua Fit the Battle," and "How Great Thou Art" – are highly regarded by collectors. Each record and sleeve: $150–200

### In-store material

RCA did a wonderful job of supplying record shops and other stores that carried Elvis's records and tapes with in-store advertising. This material included poster advertisements, mobiles, rack dividers, postcards, catalogs, standees, photographs, calendars, and record displays.

The posters that were distributed to be hung in record stores to advertise Elvis's latest 45 or LP release were, on the whole, very striking. They are similar to the movie-related advertisements in the sense that they were intended first and foremost to catch the attention of prospective customers and then to impart information. Two of these posters are especially notable. These are the advertisements for the *Elvis Christmas Special*, which was to be broadcast over Christmas 1967, and for the *Elvis Comeback Special*, broadcast in December 1968 and sponsored by the Singer Company.

ABOVE: **A "Promised Land" mobile. Mobile displays were designed to hang from the ceilings of record stores or other retail outlets. The reverse side of this mobile advertises "Aloha from Hawaii," "Recorded Live on Stage in Memphis," and "Having Fun on Stage."** $50–100

ABOVE: **An in-store
advertising display for the
promotion of "Elvis Golden
Records" (volume 2):
"50,000,000 Elvis fans can't
be wrong."**
**$150–250**

LEFT: **A Christmas album
record store advertisement.
This RCA display stand-up
promoted Elvis's Camden
series by advertising his
latest Christmas album.
The stand-up measures 15 x
20 inches.**
**$25–40**

# RCA ADVERTISING

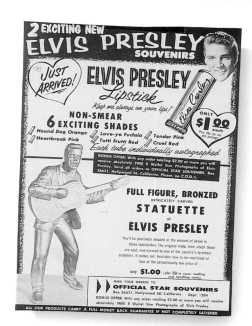

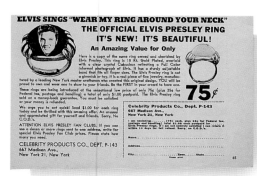

LEFT: **Advertisements also ran in fan magazines of 1956–57 promoting merchandise offered on Elvis, which carried the 1956 Elvis Presley Enterprises copyright.**

RIGHT: **The *Perfect for Parties* extended play was used as promotional enticement by RCA for their upcoming line of record albums. The extended play 45RPM offers an introduction by Elvis making reference to a song from his second long-playing album entitled *Elvis*, and he also introduces five other songs recorded by different artists.**

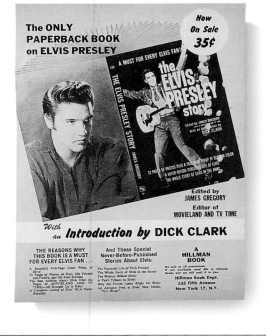

ABOVE: **Elvis Presley record player advertisement. RCA first announced the two models of Elvis Presley record players featuring Elvis's gold inlaid signature on the top in October 1956.**

LEFT: **Elvis Presley story advertisement. This advertisement was used to promote the first book about Elvis Presley to be published. The book featured articles from *Movieland* and *TV Time* magazines, and was edited by James Gregory.**

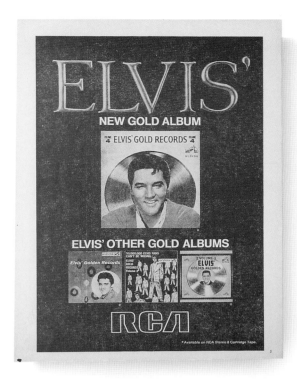

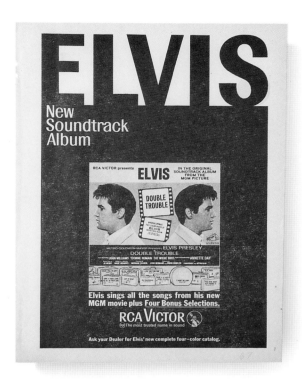

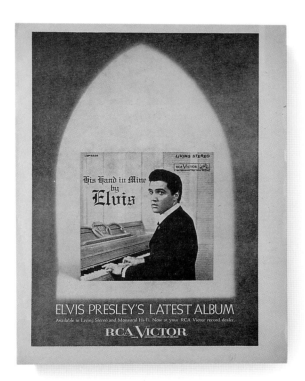

ABOVE: **Advertisements used to promote the soundtracks from Elvis movies.**

## Postcards

Another effective way of advertising and promoting the singer was through the use of postcards. These were especially directed toward the holiday seasons, especially Christmas and Easter, but they were also made for the Las Vegas concerts and other special events.

The Christmas postcards included a seasonal greeting from Elvis and the Colonel, who was usually, but not always, dressed as Santa Claus. Christmas cards were produced for 1957, 1958, 1959, 1960, 1961, 1963, 1966, 1967, 1968, 1971, 1972, 1973, 1974, and 1975, those dating from the 1950s and 1960s being the most highly regarded and those from 1957 and 1958 being especially desirable and holding the highest value. There are two versions of the 1959 card: one features a message from Western Union and the other is blank.

Easter cards were produced in 1966, 1967, 1968, and 1969. These showed a colorful close-up picture of Elvis, and on the whole they are easy to find. Two versions of the 1967 and 1968 were produced. One version of the 1967 card has an advertisement for the album "How Great Thou Art"; the other version is blank on the back. One version of the 1968 card has an advertisement for the movie *Stay Away Joe*, which was released in that year, while the back of the other version is blank.

Also of interest to collectors of postcards is the 1969 Singer card, which had the dual purpose of advertising the re-run in that year of the *Elvis Comeback Special*, originally broadcast on December 3, 1968, and sponsored by the Singer Company, and of advertising Elvis's live performance at the International Hotel, Las Vegas. Postcards from the period when Elvis was performing in Las Vegas or at Lake Tahoe coupled with advertisements for his later record release are also keenly sought.

RIGHT AND BELOW: **This postcard, issued in 1969, had the dual purpose of advertising Elvis's live performances at the International Hotel, Las Vegas, and the forthcoming re-run of his "'68 Comeback" special. The re-run was broadcast on August 17, 1969. Each card $25–30**

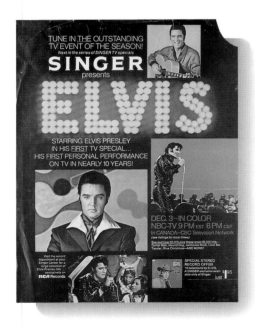

LEFT: **Singer Show Advertisement. $20–30**

LEFT: **Singer Show
Advertisement.**
**$10–15**

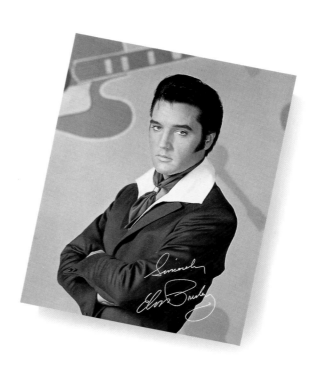

LEFT: **"Singer Presents Elvis
Singing 'Flaming Star' and
Others."**
**$40–50**

RIGHT: **This promotional
photograph was distributed
by Singer stores to patrons
who bought the "Singer
Presents Elvis Singing
'Flaming Star' and Others"
album. A much rarer
variation of the back of the
picture contained the
advertisement "Presented
by Singer Company" at the
bottom.**
**$85–100**

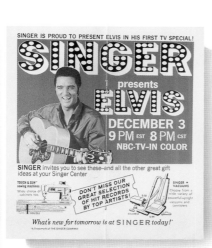

LEFT: **This beautiful,
specially made catalog, of
which the front cover,
center spread, and back are
shown, contained
information on the
television stations that
would be showing Elvis's
first TV special. It was
sponsored by the Singer
Company. The television
special, known today as The
Comeback Special, was
originally shown on NBC on
December 3, 1968.**
**$50–75**

# CHRISTMAS CARDS

1959 ($50)

1957 ($125)

1958 ($100)

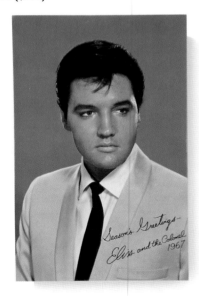

1968 ($30)

1966 ($40)

1967 ($20)

1973 ($25)

1974 ($25)

48

1960 ($50)

1961 ($40)

1963 ($50)

1971 ($25)

1972 ($20)

1975 ($20)

Another promotion by RCA was the distribution of Christmas cards. The cards illustrated were not the personal cards sent out by Elvis and the Colonel to close friends and loved ones. Rather, these cards were made for commercial purposes and distributed to business associates. The rarest card by far is the one produced in 1957; next rarest is the one sent out in 1958. All of these cards are, however, eagerly collected. None of the cards illustrated was ever included in an album. When they were, they were referred to as "bonus photos."

# E A S T E R   C A R D S

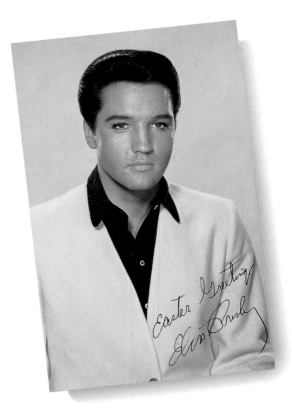

1966

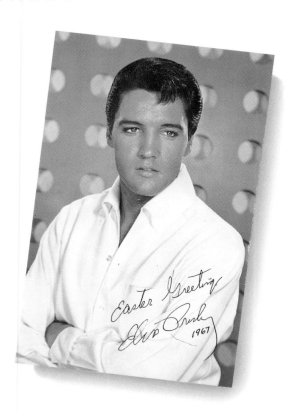

1967

Easter cards were another promotional avenue explored by RCA. The cards, which featured attractive close-up shots of Elvis, began in 1966 and appeared annually until 1969. There are two versions of the reverse sides of the 1967 and 1968 cards. One version of the 1967 card features an advertisement by RCA for the "How Great Thou Art" album. The other version is blank on the reverse. One version of the 1968 card has an advertisement for the movie *Stay Away, Joe* on the reverse; the other version has nothing on the back. Each card: $10–20

1968

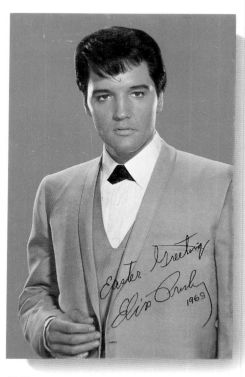

1969

# PERFORMANCE POSTCARDS

RCA distributed postcards to promote Elvis's live performances in Las Vegas and Lake Tahoe as well as to advertise his records and tapes. The postcard illustrated on the left gave information on Elvis's appearances at the Sahara Tahoe on May 4–20, 1973. The card second to the left was originally distributed in 1972. The card featuring the two close-ups of Elvis was issued in 1970 for the shows running from August 10 to September 7 at the International Hotel in Las Vegas. The card at far right features an advertisement by RCA for Elvis "Worldwide 50 Gold Award Hits" (volume 1).
Each card: $25–35

*I am a loyal Elvis Fan*

*I collect all of his records and pictures and see all of his movies*

signature

LEFT: **This is supposedly the first insert ever issued as a bonus photo with an album. The card, which measures 2¼ x 3¾ inches, bears the inscription "I am a loyal Elvis fan." It may have been inserted in "Touch of Gold" or in "Elvis is Back."** **$50–75**

## Bonus Photos

Elvis fans were often given a bonus photograph of the singer when they bought many of the albums. These photos were inserted inside the album sleeve.

It is thought that the first of these bonus photos was a small card, 2¼ x 3¾ inches, with a picture of Elvis bearing the words "Loyal Elvis Fan," which was inserted in some of the "Touch of Gold" EPs. The same insert is said to have been included in some of the issues of the "Elvis is Back" LP.

Many albums included bonus photos, but the following titles are the most popular among collectors: "It Happened at the World's Fair," "Girls! Girls! Girls!," "Harum Scarum," "Frankie and Johnny," "Spinout," "Double Trouble," "Clambake," "Speedway," "From Elvis in Memphis," "From

RIGHT: **There were three versions of the bonus photo for "Girls! Girls! Girls!" Not illustrated here is one featuring Colonel Parker dressed as Santa Claus and standing next to a snowman.**

**45RPM singles listing on the back: $100–125**
**Album listing on the back: $100–125**
**Seasons Greetings message from Elvis and the Colonel on the back: $300–350**

ABOVE: **Two other versions (in addition to those illustrated) of the bonus photos for the double album**

**"From Memphis to Vegas/From Vegas to Memphis" were issued. Each photo: $30–35**

Memphis to Vegas/From Vegas to Memphis," "Burning Love," and "Separate Ways."

Four different black and white bonus prints, each measuring 8 x 10 inches, were produced for "From Memphis to Vegas/From Vegas to Memphis," and everyone who bought a copy of the double album got two of the four different bonus photos.

There is some controversy about two photographs that may or may not have been bonus photos. The first is a black and white photo, measuring 8 x 10 inches, of Elvis in his army uniform, including his hat. Many keen and knowledgeable collectors believe that this was the bonus included with "King Creole." The second photograph about which there is some dispute is a color photograph, 8 x 10 inches, with the words "Sincerely Elvis Presley" in the lower right-hand corner. The photograph, which looks as if it were taken in 1962 or 1963, is thought by many

collectors to have been the bonus photo for "Elvis Golden Records" (volume 4). It has been stated quite categorically in another publication that neither of these albums – "King Creole" and "Elvis Golden Records" (volume 4) – contained a bonus photograph. However, other collectors, including this author, believe that the photographs were distributed to record stores to be given away to purchasers of the albums.

An important bonus promotion by RCA was the large – 16 x 20 inches – color print of the painting of the singer by June Kelly. This print was given away by record stores in the 1960s at about the time that the "Roustabout" and "Girl Happy" albums were released. The print has been reissued, but the modern version can be identified by its black border.

## Catalogs

Another popular subject for collectors are the catalogs

# B O N U S   P H O T O S

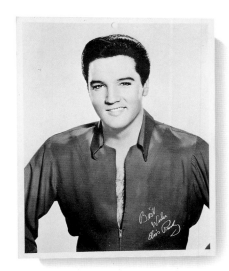

ABOVE: **This photograph was distributed at many retail stores at the time the "Viva Las Vegas" extended play and the "Kissin' Cousins" long-play were released. Each card: $25–30**

ABOVE: **"Separate Ways" (Camden) $15–20**

ABOVE: **"Wonderful World of Christmas" $20–25**

ABOVE: **"Spinout" $45–55**

ABOVE: **"Double Trouble" $35–45**

ABOVE: **"Memories of Christmas" $5–10**

ABOVE: **"Harum Scarum" $45–55**

RIGHT: **"Frankie and Johnny" $50–60**

LEFT: **"Elvis Country"**
$20–25

RIGHT: **"From Elvis in Memphis"**
$25–35

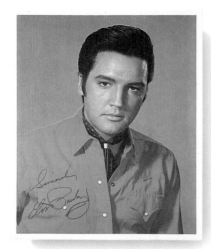

ELVIS PRESLEY

Exclusive RCA Victor
Recording Artist

BELOW: **This may be the bonus photo for "Elvis Golden Records" (volume 4).**
$150–200

ABOVE: **This may be the bonus photo distributed with the album "King Creole."**
$100–150

ABOVE: **"Clambake"**
$40–50

These bonus photos were included with the records indicated. It is possible that, rather than actually being inserted with the records, the photos were distributed to the record stores and given away when the record was bought.

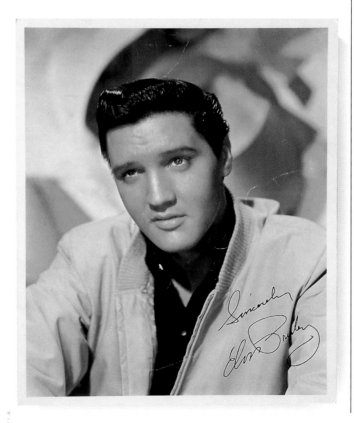

STARRING IN "KING CREOLE"

A HAL WALLIS PRODUCTION — A PARAMOUNT PICTURE

LEFT: The purpose of this 1958 wallet-size black and white photograph promoting *King Creole* is unclear. Many eager collectors believe that it was given away by record stores with the purchase of either volume 1 or volume 2 of the extended play "King Creole." Another theory is that it was given away with copies of "Elvis Sails," the extended play of the interview. Another possibility is that it was given away by movie theaters as part of the promotion of the movie. $45–60

BELOW: Christmas Special 1967. This catalog was used to promote the Elvis Christmas Special that was broadcast on December 3 and 10, 1967. $50–75

of Elvis's records and tapes. The first listing of the singer's records was issued by RCA in the form of a picture card in 1956. On one side of the card was a photograph of Elvis, while his recordings were listed on the other side. The first booklet-type catalog was distributed in 1959, and several followed after this. Many were in full color, and especially collectible are the record catalogs dating from the 1950s and 1960s. Special catalogs were produced for the 1967 *Elvis Christmas Special* and for the Singer-sponsored *Elvis Comeback Special*.

### Special Promotions

In 1956 RCA had a special promotion when it advertised the sale of two different models of record player, each style bearing Elvis's signature. One model was designed just to play 45 RPM records, but the other was a four-speed player. On both, the singer's signature was stamped in gold on the top. The purchaser of the 45 RPM player would receive a copy

ELVIS'

CHRISTMAS SPECIAL

SUNDAY, DECEMBER 3 & DECEMBER 10, 1967

GIVE ELVIS FOR CHRISTMAS

# RCA CATALOGS

ABOVE: **1967 and 1965** record catalogs $25–35

BELOW: **1969 record** catalog and 1968 record and tape catalog $25–30

ABOVE: **1959 record catalog** $50–75

LEFT: **1971 and 1970 record** catalogs $15–25

ABOVE AND LEFT: **1972** and 1973 record catalogs $15–25

LEFT: **1966 Stereo cartridge** tapes $25–30

**RCA** distributed various catalogs throughout the years in order to keep fans and retail outlets up to date with exactly what was available on record and tape. The catalogs were issued on the reverse of photographs or in the form of more detailed booklets.

of SPD-22, an extended play with eight songs on two
records, as a special bonus. Purchasers of the four-
speed player would receive SPD-23, an extended play
with 12 songs on three records. The four-speed model
also had an instruction manual with a copy of Elvis's
autograph on the front cover.

## Pocket Calendars

Another notable promotion by RCA occurred in 1963
with the issuing of the first Elvis pocket calendar, a
practice that was to continue for the next 18 years
(the last one appeared in 1980). Each calendar
featured a color photograph of Elvis on the front,
while the calendar itself and RCA's logo were printed
on the back. These calendars became especially
popular among collectors after Elvis's death.

In 1980 RCA issued authentic reproductions of
the entire set of 18 calendars. These were offered in a
blue, open-ended container, featuring the RCA logo
and bearing the legend: "By popular demand – The
1963–1980 wallet calendars." These reproductions

were produced by Boxcar Enterprises, Inc., and bore a 1979 copyright. The greatest problem facing collectors of these calendars is that the reproductions are almost identical to the originals, especially the later originals dating from 1972 to 1980. It is possible to distinguish the earlier reproductions (1963 to 1971) by slight variations in the color on the calendar side.

The most highly valued of all the pocket calendars is the one produced for 1963, and this is, perhaps, the easiest to distinguish from the 1980 reproduction. The clarity and color of the photograph, combined with the deep, rich red of the calendar, are quite distinctive.

This particular calendar is also slightly smaller than the reproduction version. The colors of the original calendars issued for 1964 to 1968, are also recognizably more vibrant than the reproductions.

Collectors should be aware that the value of the original pocket calendars has fallen sharply since the reproductions appeared. Among the other promotional items distributed by RCA were T-shirts, button badges, balloons, lei medallions, mugs, pens, tote bags, and much, much more.

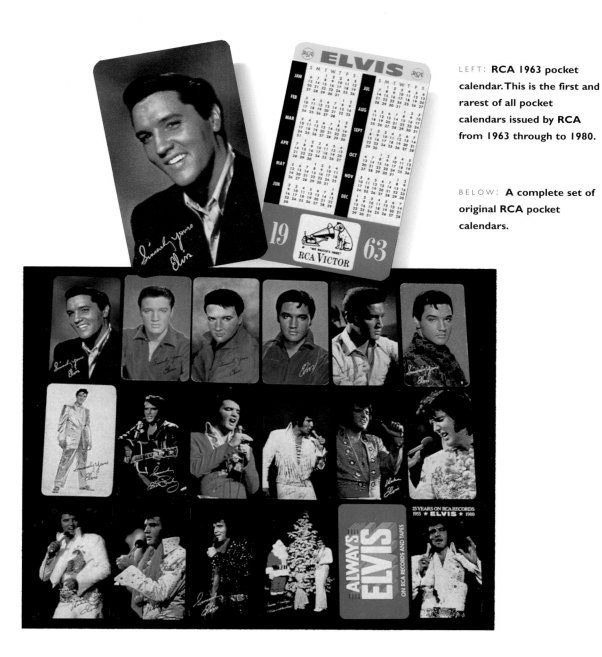

LEFT: **RCA 1963 pocket calendar. This is the first and rarest of all pocket calendars issued by RCA from 1963 through to 1980.**

BELOW: **A complete set of original RCA pocket calendars.**

YOUNG AND BEAUTIFUL
Words and Music by AARON SCHROEDER and ABNER SILVER
as Recorded by ELVIS PRESLEY on RCA Victor
ELVIS PRESLEY
Jailhouse Rock
GLADYS MUSIC, INC.
HILL AND RANGE SONGS, INC.
PRICE 50¢ IN U.S.A.
I Don't Care If The Sun Don't Shine
Words and Music by MACK DAVID
Featured by Elvis Presley
FAMOUS MUSIC CORPORATION · 1619 Broadway · New York City, N.Y.
Price 60¢

# COLLECTING
# SHEET
# MUSIC

Collectors of sheet music have an almost endless number of subjects on which to focus – everything from historical issues to social life, politics, and entertainment. Most collectors base their collections around a particular subject or topic, although collections can be built up on the basis of the composer, the kind or style of the music, and the kind of art used on the cover. The illustration used on the cover of each example of sheet music is vitally important to most collectors.

Collectors of Elvis sheet music have a lot to choose from, with over 400 song titles available. Although collections may be based on other criteria, many are especially interested in the vast number of photographs of Elvis that appeared on the sheet music over the years. This is a field of great interest to both the established collector and to the novice, for it is possible to build up a good collection without too great expenditure. It is also one of the few areas where it is often possible to find better deals in secondhand stores or ordinary collectors' fairs than at ones that concentrate exclusively on Elvis.

Although there is such a diversity of choice, you will often find the same photograph was used on more than one song title. This is especially but not exclusively the case with songs from the movies. For example, the covers of the sheet music of the songs from *G.I. Blues* are all very similar.

Popular photographs of Elvis are sometimes used on the covers of several songs from about the same date. Sometimes these are the songs from a movie, but sometimes the same photograph is used on the sheet music of songs from albums. For example, the songs for "Kiss Me Quick," "Follow That Dream," and "Just Tell Her Jim Said Hello" have similar cover illustrations.

The converse is also true, and collectors will find the same song with different cover illustrations. "Too

**"Blue Suede Shoes".**
$20–25

**"His Hand in Mine".**
$25–30

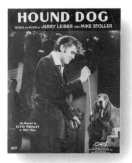

**"Hound Dog".**
$30–40

**"Heartbreak Hotel".**
$25–35

**"I Got Stung".**
$20–25

**"Such an Easy Question"**
$10–20

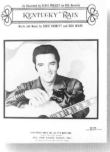

**"Kentucky Rain".**
$10–20

**"You Don't Have to Say Y**
**Love Me"** $10–15

"My Wish Came True".
$20–25

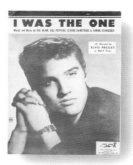

"I Was the One".
$20–25

"Flaming Star".
$20–25

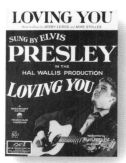

"Loving You".
$25–30

"Young and Beautiful".
$25–30

"Don't Be Cruel".
$25–35

"Clean up Your Own Back
Yard"
$10–15

"Clambake".
$10–15

"Do You Know Who I Am".
$10–15

"It's Midnight".
$10–15

"Moody Blue".
$10–15

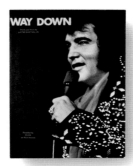

"Way Down".
$10–15

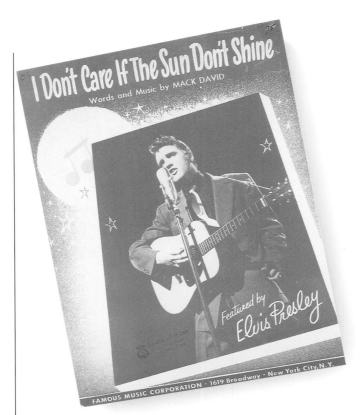

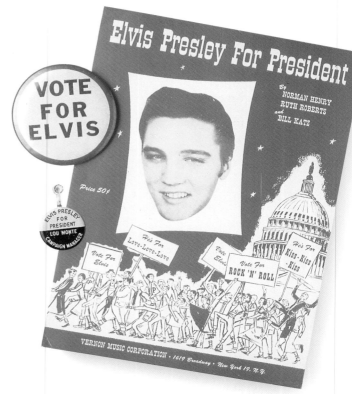

Much" and "Good Luck Charm" can both be found in different versions.

Among the most eagerly sought sheet music is that relating to the songs from early in Elvis's recording career. Highly valued songs include "Good Rockin' Tonight," "Ready Teddy," the colorful "Old Shep," and a rare "Blue Hawaii" with a cover illustration resembling the movie advertisements.

Another interesting cover illustration is the cartoon likeness of Elvis used on the sheet music for "Burning Love." This cartoon effect is reminiscent of the Beatles' animated characters in their movie, *Yellow Submarine.*

The rarest item of sheet music as far as collectors of Elvis memorabilia are concerned is not of a song recorded by Elvis, however, but a song about Elvis – "Elvis Presley for President," which was performed by Lou Monte. The song was produced in 1956, the year of a presidential election, and the sheet music was published by Vernon Music Corp. of New York City. It originally sold for 50 cents. One of the few copies known to exist recently sold for $100.

Of special interest to some collectors are the pieces of sheet music of the songs that represent Elvis's poorest efforts as a recording artist. Most of these songs were recorded for the sound tracks of the movies in which he starred, and among the lesser known titles are "Ito Eats," "Yoga is as Yoga Does," "Petunia, the Gardener's Daughter," "Shake That Tambourine," "Queenie Wahine's Papaya," and "He's Your Uncle, Not Your Dad." The sheet music for these songs is generally hard to find, largely because of the poor demand when the songs were originally issued. However, as with so much other Elvis-related material, interest in them has increased over the years, and they are now sought after.

Whether you choose to concentrate on the sheet music of the songs from Elvis's early career or the songs from the movies, or whether you prefer to build your collection around the different styles of cover illustration, there is no doubt that this is an interesting and rewarding area.

Remember that you must store and display sheet music carefully. The inks that were used on the cover illustrations often bleed, so interleave them with acid-free paper and store them flat, away from direct light and changes in temperature.

BELOW: **Two song books that contain many of Elvis's popular songs are *We Call on Him* and *The Elvis Presley Album of Juke Box Favorites*. The first of these is a collection of gospel songs** recorded by Elvis, and the book, which was published in 1968, contains 32 pages. *The Elvis Presley Album of Juke Box Favorites* **contains many of the early songs recorded by Elvis.**

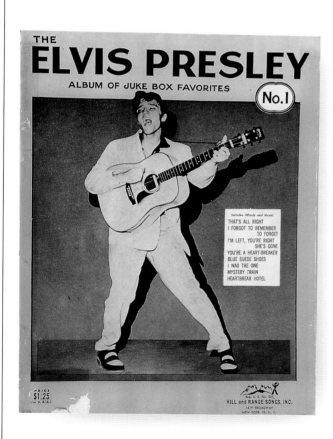

ABOVE: ***The Elvis Presley Album of Juke Box Favorites***
**$50–75**

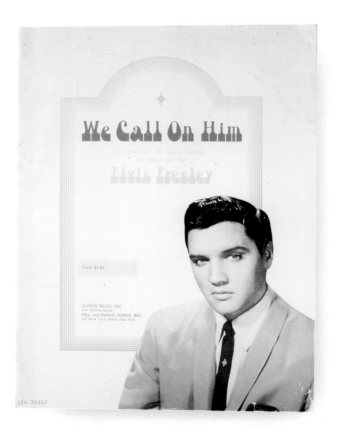

ABOVE: ***We Call on Him***
**$30–40**

COMMUNI

exclusive: MOVIELAND'S NEXT GREAT LOVER!

# elvis presley
IN HOLLYWOOD

15¢

over 70 photos!

FIRST SCENES FROM ELVIS'
PREMIERE MOTION PICTURE

The Plain Truth About Elvis Presley

LOCAL PROGRAM LISTINGS

WEEK OF SEPTEMBER 8-14

## TV GUIDE

15¢

Elvis Presley

# CHAPTER FIVE

# ELVIS

# IN

# PRINT

arketing a book or a magazine begins with a simple process: find a subject or personality in which people are interested, write the text and take the photographs, apply the rules of demographics and marketing, then launch the publication on the world.

When the publishing world discovered Elvis Presley in 1956, it found a virtually inexhaustible source of interest to readers around the world. Elvis began to appear in print almost as soon as "Heartbreak Hotel" hit the top of the charts in 1956. The fact that this was quickly followed by more chart-toppers and that Colonel Parker launched the marketing blitz with Elvis merchandise kept his name in the public eye and fueled an ever-growing appetite for all things associated with the star.

BELOW: **The first hardback annual was the** *Elvis 1963 Special*, **which was published by Albert Hand. The first annual was, however, the softback,** *Meet Elvis*, **which was published in 1962.** *Elvis 1963 Special*: **$65–90** *Meet Elvis*: **$100–125**

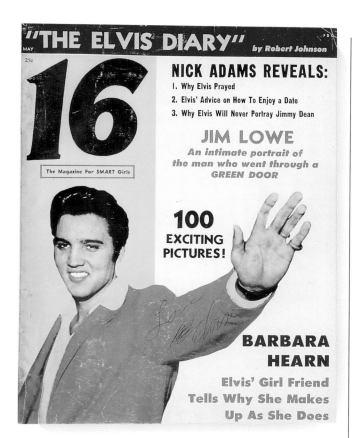

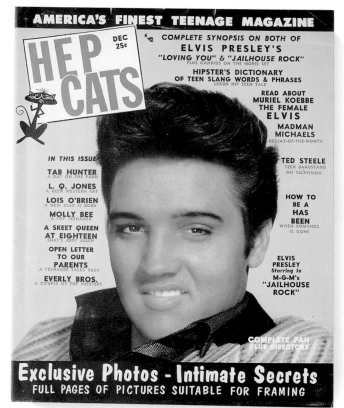

ABOVE LEFT: *16*, "The Elvis Diary," May 1957 $45–60

ABOVE: *Hep Cats*, December 1957 $70–80

This activity means that there is a wealth of magazines and fanzines available to today's collector, and although some items are expensive, much is affordable and offers a suitable area for the novice collector to begin to establish a collection.

The story of Elvis in print began in the late 1950s. There were several teen magazines on the market – *16*, *Hep Cats*, and *Teen Life*, for example – and there were magazines published by the music industry such as *Rock and Roll*, *Best Songs*, and *Songs and Stars*. Later still were mass-market magazines such as *Look*, *People*, and *TV Guide*.

Since the beginning of Elvis's career, almost every magazine and newspaper in the world has, at one time or another, written about him. His picture has adorned the covers of at least one issue of every music magazine that has been published. There is, therefore, a mass of material for the collector.

The most desirable publications are those dating from the late 1950s. For example, the edition of

*Theater Pictorial* that is devoted to *Love Me Tender* features a picture of an intensely brooding Elvis on the cover. This particular publication carries an estimated value of $250.

In 1957 Charlton Publications produced a comic book in its *Young Lovers* series entitled "The Real Elvis Presley Complete Life Story." The cover features a handsomely drawn blonde woman holding a framed black and white photograph of Elvis, who is wearing an open-necked shirt and hat. This is now considered a very rare publication, which originally sold for 10 cents, but now commands prices of $200 or more.

Also highly valued is an early publication entitled *Elvis Presley: Hero or Heel?* The cover carries a hint of what is to be found within, with the claim: "Bonus insert: Life-size Portrait in Full Color." In mint condition, a copy of the No. 1 edition of the magazine can fetch between $135 and $150.

When Gib Publish Corp. produced *Elvis Presley in Hollywood* in 1956, it could have had no idea that a publication that boasts "over 70 photos" and that originally sold for 15 cents would, some 40 years later, command a price of about $100.

Not all of these early publications command such high prices. *Rock 'n' Roll Roundup* from January 1957, which has Elvis playing his guitar on the cover, is valued at about $60, and *Record Whirl*, which had Elvis on the cover of the June 1956 edition with the question "Elvis Presley: What's All the Shouting About?," today sells for about $50.

By the 1970s, Elvis had become something of a legend. He had already sold millions of records and made Elvis Presley Enterprises and Colonel Parker wealthy. He had made RCA records a force in the music world and was still selling out concerts wherever he played – which by this time was mostly Las Vegas.

In 1971 a special edition of *Screen Stars*, "Elvis: 1971 Presley Album," featured articles with titles such as "How Elvis Went from Singer to Swinger" and "His Life Story, His Love Story and His Success Story." This originally sold for 50 cents and now carries a value of approximately $30. *Circus Magazine Pinups* devoted its third edition to Elvis, entitling it "The Elvis Years." This publication now costs about $30.

Even at the end of the decade, Elvis was still getting plenty of coverage in print. In 1976 Ideal published *Elvis: The Hollywood Years*, which is now

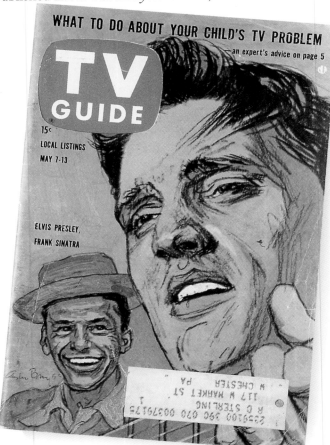

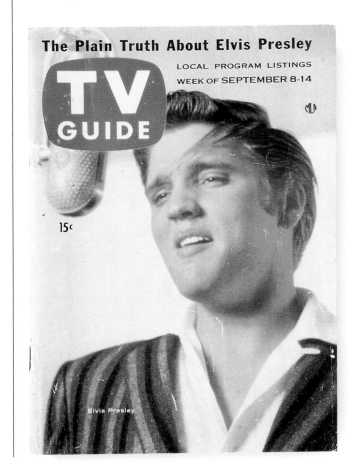

LEFT: **The first time that Elvis appeared on the cover of the *TV Guide* was for the issue dated September 8–14, 1956. $100–150**

ABOVE: **To capitalize on his return from the army, *TV Guide* for May 7–13, 1960, featured the likeness of Elvis with Frank Sinatra. Elvis's appearance as a guest on the Frank Sinatra Timex Special on May 8, 1960, marked his first TV performance since his discharge from the army. $50–70**

worth an estimated $20. May of that year saw a *Tatler* Special Issue, "Elvis: The Trials and Triumphs of the Legendary King of Rock 'n' Roll." This originally sold for $1 and now commands approximately 20 times that amount.

In 1975, when Elvis turned 40, *People* magazine was there to mark the occasion. The edition for January 13 was on the newsstands at 40 cents. It is now valued at $15–20.

National magazines were not the only publications to take note of Elvis. Both the *New York Herald Tribune* and the *Chicago Tribune* used pictures of Elvis on the covers of their weekly TV magazines, the *Herald Tribune* on June 24, 1956, and the *Chicago Tribune* on July 7, 1956. The *Washington Post* was more interested in the dying days of the Eisenhower administration, but on June 19, 1960, its Sunday

TOP: *Elvis Presley in Hollywood*, 1956, 4½ x 5½ inches $85–100

ABOVE: **One of the most attractive promotional items issued by RCA was a 1963 magazine simply entitled** *Elvis.* **This full-color picture folio magazine offers some of the very first photographs of Elvis ever produced. The first edition of** *Elvis* **included a fold-out poster measuring 11 x 21 inches. A few pages feature listings of Elvis's records, but even so, this is a first-rate magazine for those collectors who love photographs of the singer. Later issues of the magazine did not include the poster. With poster $40–50 Without poster $30–40**

ABOVE AND RIGHT: **Elvis was even the topic of conversation in the comic books** *Young Lovers* **(1957) and** *Career Girl Romances* **(1966).** *Young Lovers:* **$175–250** *Career Girl Romances:* **$90–125**

magazine featured a youthful Elvis, tending to his hair, with an article entitled, "Elvis Presley: He's fighting to stay on top."

In 1976, the singer made the Sunday magazines of two papers that were closer to home. On August 19 he was on the cover of the *Louisville Courier–Journal & Times* magazine. A week later, his home town newspaper, the *Memphis Commercial–Appeal*, featured a concert photo on its cover. Elvis

was also good for sales across the nation. *The Houston Chronicle*, the *Houston Post*, the *New York News*, and the *Long Island Sunday Press* were just a few of the Sunday supplements that featured Elvis at various times in his career. He proved so popular in Virginia that the *Roanoke Times Parade* featured Elvis at least three times in the late 1950s and early 1960s.

Elvis even inspired publications devoted solely to himself. During his career, the major and minor

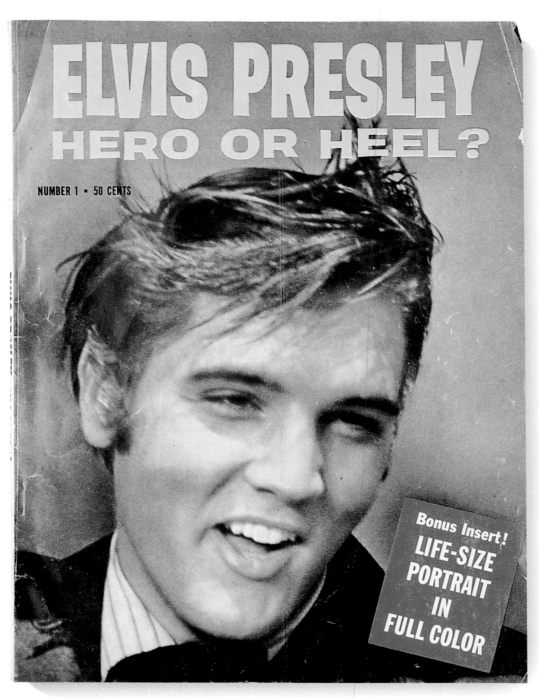

LEFT: *Elvis Presley: Hero or Heel?*, 1957
$125–140

events of his life were featured in *Elvis Monthly*, *A Century of Elvis*, and *The Elvis Pocket Handbook*. There was also *Elvis Today*, *The Elvis Encyclopedia*, and *Presley Nation*, among many others.

Getting your Presley collection under way or advancing an already established collection need not be difficult. You might begin by going to your local newspaper and asking if they have a copy of the edition for August 17, 1977 – the day Elvis died. That need be neither difficult nor expensive to obtain, and it will firmly root your collection in your own locality.

BELOW: **One of the best-ever publications on Elvis was the magazine *Elvis Monthly*, which was published in Britain, originally by the late Albert Hand. The first issue, which is illustrated at far left, appeared in February 1960. The second issue, in the center, appeared in March, and the third, right, followed a month later.**
**February 1960: $60–85**
**March 1960: $40–50**
**April 1960: $20–30**

# CHAPTER SIX

# THE MOVIES

ELVIS
PRESLEY
as he appears in
his first motion picture
Love Me Tender
from 20th CENTURY-FOX in
CINEMASCOPE

One of the most enjoyable and also one of the most flexible areas of Elvis memorabilia is the one that covers the movie-related items. During his career, Elvis appeared in 33 films, and the vast amount of movie advertising that was distributed for promoting each title was not only abundant, but artistically appealing as well.

For each of Elvis's films, from *Love Me Tender* in 1956 to the documentary *Elvis on Tour* in 1972, there were movie posters, lobby cards, film stills, press books, standees, and much for the theaters to display to promote the films. All of these movie pieces are now regarded as collectible, and they are keenly collected by both Elvis enthusiasts and movie buffs. Unfortunately, the days of sending off $1.00 to the National Screen Company in exchange for your favorite Elvis Presley poster are long gone.

BELOW: **This extremely rare special poster for *Jailhouse Rock* was not created by the National Screen Company. It carries no release date or producer, and is believed to have been made at the direction of Colonel Parker and put on the lot of the film's location. The poster is thought to have been produced before National Screen issued the original poster for the film. $700–1,200**

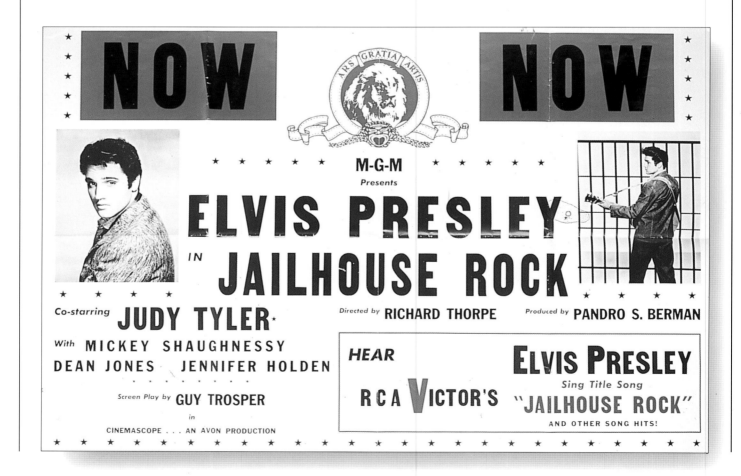

Collecting movie memorabilia not only offers a wide variety of items from which to choose, but there is also plenty of material to be attractively displayed. Collectors can concentrate on the materials associated with a specific film or group of films, or they can specialize in one or other type of material, some of which are discussed in this chapter. As with all areas of collecting, however, choose the items that you really like and that you want to have around you.

## ONE-SHEET POSTERS

Among the most popular types of movie memorabilia are the sheets of paper, 27 x 41 inches, known as one-sheet poster – that is, the standard movie poster – and one-sheets were made for all 33 of Elvis's films. The value of the one-sheet poster can largely determine the value of other promotional material for the same film. One-sheet posters were printed on light paper stock, and they were folded after printing so that they could be easily sent to movie theaters all over the country.

Sometimes, when a film was re-released for a second run, a reissue poster was made available to the cinemas. These reissue posters sometimes varied from

ABOVE: **Special invitation tickets for the press preview of** *Jailhouse Rock* (1957) **were wrapped around the standard picture sleeve, which contained the 45RPM recording of "Jailhouse Rock" backed by "Treat Me Nice." The invitation read: "You and one guest are cordially invited to the Press Preview of Elvis Presley in** *Jailhouse Rock.*"
$900–1,200

BELOW LEFT: **A one-sheet for** *Change of Habit* (1969), **the singer's last dramatic film.**
$50–75

BELOW: **An original one-sheet, 27 x 41 inches, for** *King Creole*, **considered by many critics to be the best movie Elvis made.**
$200–400

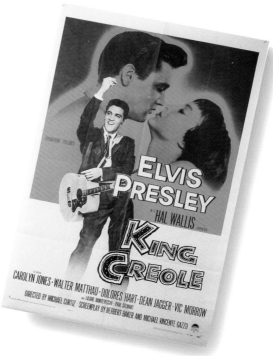

the originals. For example, the reissue poster for *King Creole* had different graphics from the original version. At least two Elvis films had more than one version of the original one-sheet poster – *Viva Las Vegas* and *Elvis on Tour*.

Posters that were larger than the one-sheets were also produced for advertising purposes. These are the three-sheet, six-sheet, and 24-sheet size.

The three-sheet posters, which measure 41 x 81 inches, were printed on light paper and supplied in two or three sections. They were produced for all 33 of Elvis's films. Depending on the popularity of the film concerned and the quality of the illustration, the three-sheet poster can command a higher price than the one-sheet for the same film. *Jailhouse Rock* and *Viva Las Vegas* are examples of this. On the other hand, the one-sheet can be more expensive than the three-sheet if the quality of the artwork is not good and if the film is not one of the more popular titles.

Six-sheet posters, which measure 81 x 81 inches, were printed on lightweight paper. Again, depending on the graphics of the poster and the popularity of the film, they can command high prices. The size of the six-sheet in relation to the available room space required to display it properly can discourage some collectors. The six-sheets for all the movies were sometimes not illustrated in the press books, but they could be ordered through National Screen. Six-sheet posters are considered to be very scarce.

The large 24-sheet posters, which measure 9 x 13½ feet, were printed on lightweight paper, and, according to the press books, they were made for all of Elvis's films except *Elvis on Tour*. They were intended for billboard advertising, and unless a collector has a museum or some large public area – a café, perhaps – in which they can be displayed, they are not suitable for most collectors. These posters are extremely rare, largely because so many were destroyed.

ABOVE: **A three-sheet, 41 x 81 inches, for *G.I. Blues*** $125–250

## WINDOW CARDS, INSERT POSTERS, AND HALF-SHEET POSTERS

Some of the most popular items of movie memorabilia are the window cards, insert posters, and half-sheet posters.

Window cards, which measure 14 x 22 inches, were printed on heavier paper than the posters. In simple financial terms, they offer the collector a tremendous saving in terms of cost and framing. They are ideal for displaying in small rooms, and they blend well with inserts and half-sheet posters. One problem that many collectors have with the window card is that most have writing along the top. Most collectors prefer "clean" cards, although the information about the venue and date does add to the nostalgia of the

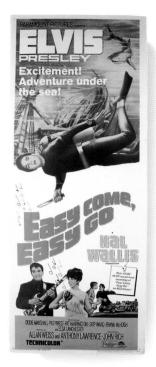

ABOVE: **An insert, 14 x 36 inches, for *Easy Come, Easy Go*** $50–75

ABOVE: **An insert, 14 x 36 inches, for *Clambake*** $50–75

ABOVE: **Although it reproduces the original graphics, this insert for *King Creole*, measuring 14 x 36 inches, is regarded as a reissue.** $175–250

ABOVE: **An insert, 14 x 36 inches, for *Flaming Star*** $100–150

ABOVE: **An insert, 14 x 36 inches, for *The Trouble with Girls*** $50–75

ABOVE: **An insert, 14 x 36 inches, for *Charro!*** $60–90

piece – and that is, after all, what the cards were originally designed to show. Many of the window cards designed for Elvis's movies were bright and colorful, and at least two – those for *Loving You* and *Frankie and Johnny* – used a different illustration for the window card from the illustrations used on the other posters advertising those films.

Insert posters, which were 14 x 36 inches, were printed on fairly heavy paper. Many of these small posters were extremely attractive, sometimes superior to the larger posters used to advertise the same film. The insert for *Love Me Tender*, Elvis's first film, with its photographic approach, compares very favorably with the illustrative design used on the one-sheet. These posters look very impressive when displayed on a wall, and their vertical size is a good contrast with the other posters, especially the half-sheets. Although most insert posters were originally folded, it is possible to find examples that were rolled.

BELOW: **A half-sheet, 22 x 28 inches, for** *Tickle Me*
**$60–90**

BELOW: **A half-sheet, 22 x 28 inches, for** *Viva Las Vegas*
**$150–200**

Half-sheet posters are also sometimes known as lobby photo cards or display posters. They measured 22 x 28 inches and were printed on heavy paper. The half-sheet was available in two original styles for *Loving You, Jailhouse Rock,* and *King Creole,* and an original reissue with a different illustration was prepared for the re-release of *King Creole.* The posters were not always changed when a film was re-released, but look in the lower right-hand corner. An R indicates that the poster accompanied a re-release. The letter R will be followed by a number followed by a slash or oblique, followed by another number. These numbers represent the year in which the film was re-released, followed by an identification number indicating the number of films the National Screen Service had printed during the course of that particular year. An original poster will not have the R.

## POSTERS

Some of the more stylish and colorful pieces of movie material are the posters that measure 30 x 40 inches and 40 x 60 inches. These were printed on durable card stock and may have been made for all 33 films. Although the press books do not indicate that these posters were printed for some movies, the author has personally seen the larger size for *Loving You, King Creole, It Happened at the World's Fair,* and *Kissin' Cousins.* There may have been more than one style of these particular posters. For example, at least two of the larger size are known for *Wild in the Country,* and

BELOW LEFT: **This 40 x 60-inch poster for *Blue Hawaii* has a different color scheme from the other posters promoting this film. $150–300**

BELOW: **A 40 x 60-inch poster for *Roustabout* $100–150**

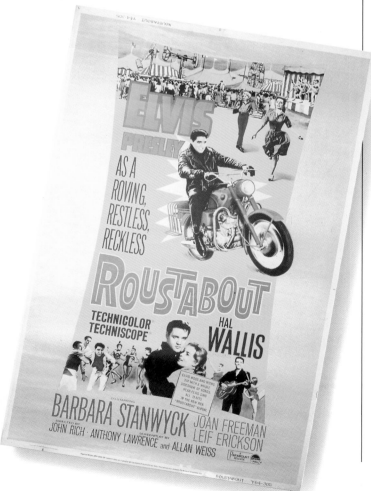

several different designs of the larger size are believed to have been produced for *Follow That Dream*. These posters, with their wonderful colors, are undoubtedly among the most attractive of the movie-related items, but some collectors may be deterred from acquiring them because of their size. The larger ones in particular are difficult to display adequately.

## LOBBY CARDS

Many collectors rank lobby cards among the most popular of all movie-related collectibles. Eight lobby cards were produced for each movie. They all measure 11 x 14 inches and were printed on cardboard. Because they illustrate different scenes from the movie, they are sometimes known as scene cards. The title, credits, and release date of the film are printed along the base of the card, and their value usually depends on whether they show a close-up or a distant scene. Clarity and the significance of the scene in the film are also important considerations. The dance scene from *Jailhouse Rock* is, for example, one of the most keenly collected, but cards that do not feature Elvis or any of the other major stars or that lack graphic appeal are often referred to as "dead" cards.

Sets of eight lobby cards for *Love Me Tender*, *Loving You*, *Jailhouse Rock,* and *King Creole* were reissued. The reissued cards for *Love Me Tender* showed the same scenes as the original ones, although the sequence was changed. The reissue sets for *Loving You* and *King Creole* are among the rarest of all lobby cards. In common with other reissue material, the cards bore the letter R, preceding the date the movie was released in the lower right-hand corner. Three of Elvis's films – *Love Me Tender*, *Jailhouse Rock,* and *Flaming Star* – had title cards. These have a poster-like effect and are regarded as very desirable.

BELOW AND RIGHT: **Lobby cards, each 11 x 14 inches, for *Viva Las Vegas*.**
**$40–60**

RIGHT: **A lobby card, 11 x 14 inches, for the reissue of *King Creole*.**
**$50–65**

# LOBBY CARDS

RIGHT: **A lobby card, 11 x 14 inches, for** *G.I. Blues*
**$35–50**

LEFT: **A lobby card, 11 x 14 inches, for** *Wild in the Country*
**$30–40**

RIGHT: **A lobby card, 11 x 14 inches, for** *Blue Hawaii*
**$35–50**

BELOW: **Lobby cards, each
11 x 14 inches, for *That's the
Way It Is*
Each card: $30–40**

ABOVE: **A lobby card, 11 x
14 inches, for *Follow that
Dream*
$20–25**

ABOVE: **A lobby card, 11 x
14 inches, for *Loving You*
$65–85**

## O T H E R   M O V I E   M E M O R A B I L I A

Quite possibly the rarest of all the movie poster advertisements are the ones that are known as door panels. These measure 201 x 60 inches, and they were made for only a few of Elvis's films.

"Standees" are another rare and highly collectible item. These featured a posing Elvis on heavy-duty cardboard. They were usually between 5 and 6 feet tall. Similar were the pieces known as "hi-rise standees," which were used for many of the films. These were usually enlargements of the one-sheet poster, and they stood in the front or lobby of the theater to promote the forthcoming film.

BELOW: **These are the only three title cards from the 33 films that Elvis made. They resemble posters, and they have a higher value than lobby cards.**
*Flaming Star*: $75–90
*Jailhouse Rock*: $250–300
*Love Me Tender*: $200–250

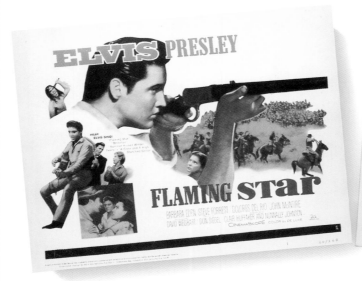

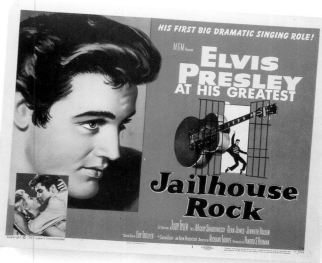

LEFT: **A "standee" for** *Love Me Tender.* This is a very rare movie-related item and highly collectible.
$800–1,200

Catch his fun-picture of them all
--with all these catchy songs!
"Follow That Dream"
"Sound Advice"
"What A Wonderful Life"
"I'm Not The Marrying H
"Angel"

ELVIS PRESLEY in FOLLOW THAT DREAM

Join the fun! It's the chase that changed the face of sunny Florida!

CO-STARRING ARTHUR O'CONNELL

ANNE HELM · JOANNA MOORE · JACK KRUSCHEN
DIRECTED BY GORDON DOUGLAS · SCREENPLAY BY CHARLES LEDERER · RICHARD POWELL
PRODUCED BY DAVID WEISBART
BASED ON THE NOVEL PIONEER, GO HOME! · RELEASED THRU UNITED ARTISTS

HALF BREED

TORN BETWEEN TWO LOYALTIES ...TWO LOVES AND FIGHTING TO SAVE THEM BOTH!

ELVIS PRESLEY FLAMING STAR

BARBARA EDEN · STEVE FORREST · DOLORES DEL RIO · JOHN McINTIRE

CINEMASCOPE® COLOR by DE LUXE

Produced by DAVID WEISBART · Directed by DON SIEGEL · Screenplay by CLAIR HUFFAKER AND NUNNALLY JOHNSON
20th CENTURY-FOX

ABOVE: **A stand-up poster for** *Follow that Dream.*
$150–250

ABOVE: **A stand-up poster for** *Flaming Star.*
$150–250

Still photographs, both black and white and color, were issued for all but three Elvis movies – those three were *Love Me Tender*, *Jailhouse Rock*, and *King Creole*. Both the black and white and the color stills measure 8 x 10 inches. Many of the black and white photos and all of the color stills feature the title and credits along the bottom of each picture. Unlike the lobby cards, no set number of stills was issued with each movie, although there were normally between 8 and 12 color stills, but anything from 10 to 20 black and white stills, depending on the film. Because of the sharpness of the print and attractive appearance of the color stills, many collectors prefer them to lobby cards.

ELVIS PRESLEY as he appears in his first motion picture
Love Me Tender
from 20th CENTURY-FOX in CINEMASCOPE

# MOVIE STILLS

LEFT: *Girls! Girls! Girls!*, color still, 8 x 10 inches.
$10–14

BELOW: *Stay Away Joe*, color still, 8 x 10 inches.
$9–12

BELOW: *Live a Little, Love a Little*, color still, 8 x 10 inches.
$9–12

BELOW: *It Happened at the World's Fair*, color still, 8 x 10 inches.
$10–14

ABOVE: *Fun in Acapulco,*
color still, 8 x 10 inches.
$9–12

BELOW: *The Trouble with
Girls,* color still, 8 x
10 inches.
$9–12

ABOVE: *It Happened at the
World's Fair,* black and white
still, 8 x 10 inches.
$10–14

ABOVE: *Flaming Star,* black
and white still, 8 x 10 inches.
$9–12

ABOVE: *It Happened at the
World's Fair,* black and white
still, 8 x 10 inches.
$7–9

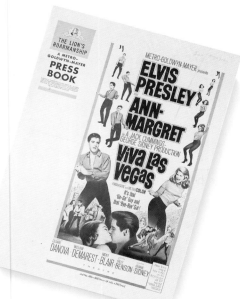

ABOVE: **The press book for**
*G.I. Blues.*
$80–110

ABOVE: **The press book for**
*Viva Las Vegas.*
$75–100

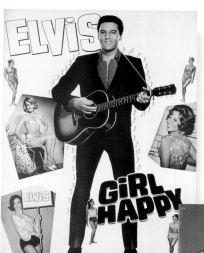

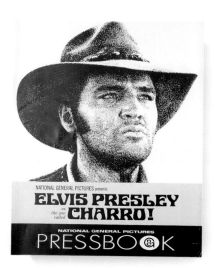

ABOVE: **The press book for**
*Girl Happy.*
$30–45

ABOVE: **The press book for**
*Charro!*
$25–35

LEFT: **The press book for**
*Elvis on Tour.*
$30–40

Press books are also very popular among collectors. A press book always appeared before the movie in order to alert the movie theater's management that the material was going to be available to promote the film. Press books also included a brief synopsis of the film, as well as outlining all the promotional displays and advertising material that would be available. The books varied in length and size. Those for *G.I. Blues*, *Loving You*, and *Love Me Tender* are the largest. Press books are generally an excellent source of reference for information on the different kinds and sizes of poster that were produced for each film, although there are exceptions. The film *Jailhouse Rock* was unusual in having an advance press book as well as an original press book, and reissue press books were produced for *King Creole* and *Flaming Star*. Intact press books command considerable premiums.

LEFT AND BELOW: **The press book for *Loving You*.** $140–175

LEFT: **The press book for *Blue Hawaii*.** $80–100

Small newspaper fliers, which are usually known as tabloid heralds, were usually purchased in bulk by theater managers to announce the imminent showing of a movie. These fliers were often given away to patrons of the cinema, but they were also distributed to record stores.

Large, colorful banners made of durable, heavy-duty cardboard were also used to promote the movies. These banners measure 24 x 82 inches, and they were often hung in the front foyer of theaters. The banners from the earliest movies are very hard to find. They look magnificent when they are displayed in a large room. No one is certain how many of these banners were produced for each film. This author has seen at least one banner that was not listed in the press book.

One type of poster that seems to be overlooked by collectors is the double bill featuring the movies *Fun in Acapulco* and *Girls! Girls! Girls!* Posters of various sizes were made available for this promotion, and there was also a press book. This is the only known "double bill" promotion known to exist, although some say that a double bill for *Flaming Star* and *Wild in the Country* may exist.

Other posters of which collectors should be aware were from the three films that were originally going to have different names – *Harum Scarum* (*Harum Holiday*), *Spinout* (*California Holiday*), and *Viva Las Vegas* (*Love in Las Vegas*). These were distributed by the National Screen Service. Poster and lobby cards with the original titles were prepared for these films, which were issued in Europe with their original titles.

Posters originating in countries other than the

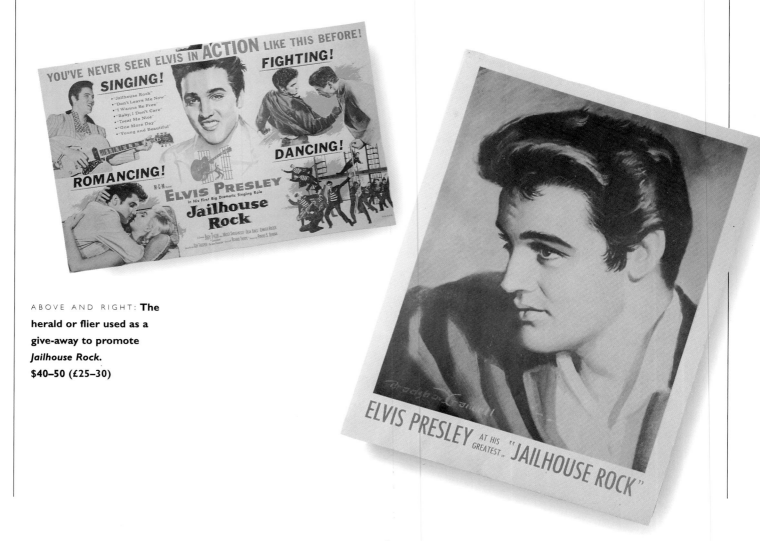

ABOVE AND RIGHT: **The herald or flier used as a give-away to promote** *Jailhouse Rock.* **$40–50 (£25–30)**

United States vary greatly in size from the U.S. equivalents, and they also tend to be printed on much lighter paper. However, the colors are often much brighter and the graphics are generally better than the U.S. versions. It is usually not possible to tell if these non-U.S. posters were for reissues or for an original release, because most of them do not bear the identification numbers and reference information found on U.S. posters. Most non-U.S. posters do not even show release dates.

The novice collector should be alert to the difference between reissue posters and reproductions. A reissue poster is an authentic movie poster made for the re-release of a film. A reproduction, on the other hand, is nothing more than an imitation or reproduction of an original poster. Reproductions are usually fairly easy to identify because their sizes are not identical with the original versions, they are also likely to be found in gift shops, and they carry the manufacturer's name.

BELOW: **The *G.I. Blues* hat, which measures 5½ x 11¹⁄₁₆ inches, and accompanying blue ticket that originally came with the hat, admitted the bearer to the movie. $100–150**

DO YOU HAVE
RCA VICTOR'S
ORIGINAL SOUNDTRACK ALBUM
OF
BLUE HAWAII
**ELVIS**
SINGS
**14 GREAT
SONGS**

LEFT AND ABOVE: **This
Hawaiian lei had the dual
purpose of promoting the
film *Blue Hawaii* and the
soundtrack album.
$125–175**

Special Photo Folio Concert Edition

# LAS VEGAS

LAS VEGAS HILTON
THE INTERNATIONAL HOTEL

SOUVENIR MENU 1972
complimentary copy

During the 1960s and 1970s, many performers regarded a show at one of the major hotels at Las Vegas, Nevada, the high point of their careers. Therefore, when Elvis decided to return to the limelight with the 1968 *Elvis Comeback Special*, it was natural that he should consider appearing in Las Vegas. It seemed, in fact, like easy money, for instead of the rigors of, a 12-city tour of New England, Presley and his entourage could make their base in a single hotel and perform in a series of concerts in just one venue.

The problem was convincing Elvis of this. Throughout his career he had always been conscious of, and remained loyal to, his roots. He also remembered his early failures at performing – the embarrassment at the Grand Ole Opry, the rejection from Arthur Godfrey, and other occasions when he had not been well received. So when Colonel Parker suggested booking a series of shows in Las Vegas for 1969, Elvis might well have recalled April and May 1956.

On April 23, 1956, the singer made his first appearance at Las Vegas. The venue was the New Frontier Hotel, and the audience consisted almost entirely of older, more conservative people, who did not take well to the young performer from Tennessee, who sang an entirely new kind of music. When one audience responded particularly coldly to his performance, Elvis told them that their lack of emotion was "pitiful." What had been booked as a four-week engagement was closed after just two weeks.

Although this experience at Las Vegas left him bitter, Elvis continued to tour. He left Nevada on May 6, happy to kick the sand from his shoes, and just seven days later, he gave two shows in St. Paul, Minnesota. The next day, May 14, he gave two more shows in La Crosse, Wisconsin, and on May 15 he was back in Memphis, where rows of police officers were needed in the Ellis Auditorium to keep the fans from rushing onto the stage. He did not return to Las Vegas for 13 years.

In July 1969, however, Colonel Parker was negotiating for Elvis's triumphant return to the desert, turning everything in the city into a means of advertising the singer's imminent arrival. On July 5 (after a brief diet), Elvis returned to Las Vegas and began rehearsing for his show at the Hilton International Hotel. This time he remembered the advice that Liberace had given him after his 1956 debacle: "Dress to please the audience." So, for his return to Las Vegas, Elvis abandoned the black leather that he had sported since the Christmas *Comeback Special* and instead he wore a black, karate-style outfit for the opening night. However, he soon pioneered the rhinestone-studded jumpsuit that became his trademark in the 1970s. He became the rhinestone cowboy, and his wardrobe matched the neon lights that shone throughout the Vegas nights. There were even rumors that the rhinestone-decorated jumpsuit weighed 40 pounds.

On July 31, 1969, Elvis appeared live on stage at the International Hotel, and the audience were treated to a polished performance from a singer who was on top of his material. No longer the gangly teenager in baggy clothes, Elvis proved he could successfully blend rock, rhythm and blues, country and gospel music into a balanced act. This performance began a series of 1,126 sold-out shows.

The first shows were in front of 2,000 people a night, with performances at 8:00 P.M. and midnight. By the end of the 29-day run, ticket receipts alone had brought in more than $1.5 million, and the International Hotel presented Elvis with a gold belt for holding "the world championship attendance record." The belt is on display in a trophy case at Graceland.

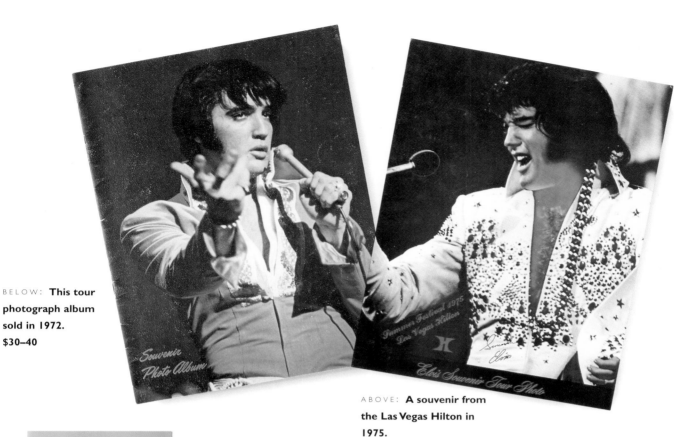

BELOW: **This tour photograph album sold in 1972. $30–40**

ABOVE: **A souvenir from the Las Vegas Hilton in 1975. $25–30**

ABOVE: **This illustration clearly demonstrates that three different versions of this program existed. The one at the top was used for concert tours, while the other two bear the logos of the International Hotel and RCA. The version with the International Hotel logo is the most desirable of the three. These programs first appeared c.1970. RCA and tour programs: $30–40 International Hotel program: $45–55**

ABOVE: **The album contains 16 black and white photographs. $30–40**

LEFT: **This special concert edition was a different size from the other tour programs – 7 x 13⅞ inches. $30–40**

But in addition to generating tremendous excitement by his live performances, Elvis's shows in Las Vegas created a whole new area for collectors. Dozens of souvenirs made exclusively for the Hilton International were available for sale in the hotel lobby, and the line included hound dogs, teddy bears, imitation straw hats, scarves, pennants, posters, and lapel badges.

Later, when Elvis started to appear at the Sahara Tahoe Hotel, the souvenirs that were offered for sale were very similar to those that had been sold at the Hilton International, but the Sahara's name was embossed on them instead.

From 1971, when Elvis began to give concert tours, merchandise specially created for the shows was sold in the lobbies of all the theaters in which he appeared. This merchandise included posters, photo albums, costume jewelry, and pennants, and many of the pieces were also later offered for sale at the Las Vegas engagements.

BELOW: **Both versions of the Special Photo Folio Concert Edition (volume 5) contain 16 pages of color. Although the programs look the same except for the color around the star, three pages in the blue version are different from the red counterpart. Each version: $25–35**

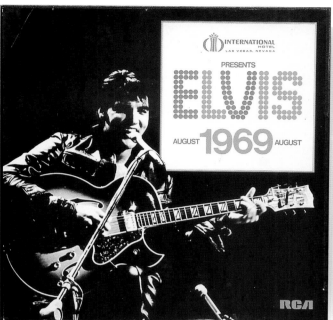

LEFT AND BELOW: **Probably
the most coveted Elvis-related
Las Vegas item is the 1969
International Hotel gift boxed
set. This set was given to
invited guests when they
attended the premier
engagement of Elvis's return to
the live stage on July 31 and
August 1, 1969. The
International Hotel also issued
a gift boxed set in 1970 to
special guests for Elvis's
opening night on January 26,
1970.
1969 boxed set and contents
complete: $900–1,200**

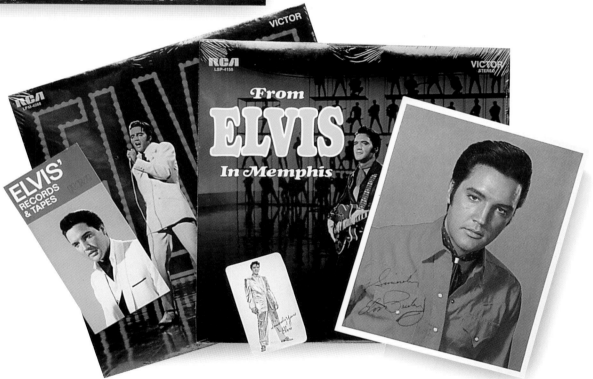

Although the merchandise available for purchase
is collected, most keen collectors prefer the associated
items that were produced for promotional and
advertising purposes, such as paper and satin banners,
complimentary shopping bags, and posters.

Many collectors specialize in menus, and
especially highly sought after are the menus from the
Las Vegas and Lake Tahoe engagements. Beginning
in 1969 and lasting until 1976, a variety of menus,

# VEGAS MENUS

ABOVE: **This menu was used for Elvis's opening engagement at the International Hotel in Las Vegas in 1969.** $350–500

ABOVE: **This black and white menu was issued in 1970 for an engagement at the International Hotel, Las Vegas.** $100–150

ABOVE: **The menu issued for the 1971 engagement at the International Hotel, Las Vegas.** $75–100

ABOVE: **The menu for January 26 to February 23, 1972.** $50–60

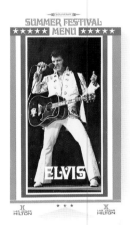

ABOVE: **The menu for the Las Vegas Hilton, August 4 to September 4, 1972.** $45–60

ABOVE: **There were two different sizes of the menu for the Las Vegas Hilton, January 26 to February 23, 1973. The one illustrated is 7 x 14 inches. The other measures 4 x 7½ inches. Large menu: $30–40 Small menu: $35–45**

ABOVE: **This menu was used for the 1975 engagement at the Las Vegas Hilton.** $45–60

ABOVE: **The menu, August 19 to September 2, 1974, for the Las Vegas Hilton.** $30–40

ABOVE: **The menu for the Sahara Tahoe Hotel, May 16–26, 1974.** $35–50

ABOVE: **The menu for the International Hotel, January 26 to February 23, 1971.** $85–100

ABOVE: **The menu for the Sahara Tahoe, July 20 to August 2, 1971.** $75–100

ABOVE: **The menu for the International Hotel, August 9 to September 6, 1971.** $45–60

ABOVE: **The menu for the Sahara Tahoe, May 4–20, 1973, is 9¾ inches across. A smaller menu, 8 inches across, was also available.** $85–100

ABOVE: **The menu for the Las Vegas Hilton, August 6 to September 3, 1973.** $30–40

ABOVE: **The menu for the Las Vegas Hilton, January 26 to February 9, 1974.** $35–50

ABOVE: **This menu, for December 2–15, 1975, measures 7 x 16⅛ inches.** $125–150

LEFT: **The Las Vegas Hilton menu, August 18–20, 1975.** $125–150

ABOVE: **This menu was issued as part of a package for a 1975 engagement at the Las Vegas Hilton. A photograph folio was included for the guests.** $50–65

ranging in size and shape, were printed. These menus were available to the guests attending an Elvis show in Las Vegas or at Lake Tahoe. Menus from the early years are especially desirable. The rarest of all are those that were made especially for the maitre d' and captains of the hotels. None of them is more highly prized, however, than the menu for Elvis's first engagement at the Las Vegas Hilton International in 1969.

Perhaps the most highly sought after of all the items of memorabilia produced for the singer's appearances at the Las Vegas Hilton International are the boxed sets that were issued to a select few in 1969 and early 1970. Both boxed sets had the same cover as the commercially released album "From Memphis to Vegas." The 1969 boxed set contained: the albums "Elvis" (the NBC-TV Special) and "Elvis in Memphis"; a nine-page letter from Elvis and Colonel Parker; a 1969 records and tape catalog; two 8 x 10-inch black and white photographs of Elvis; a 1969

BELOW: **Color postcards of the Hilton Hotel, Las Vegas. Each card: $8–15**

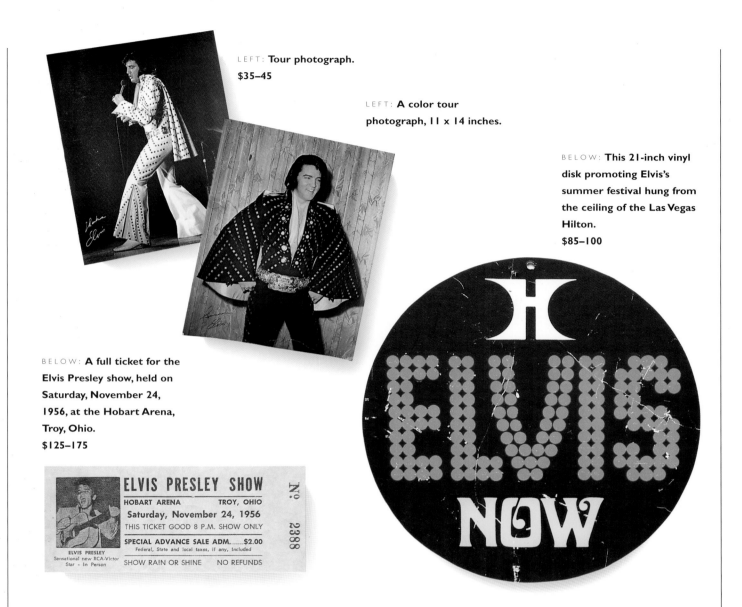

LEFT: **Tour photograph.**
**$35–45**

LEFT: **A color tour**
**photograph, 11 x 14 inches.**

BELOW: **This 21-inch vinyl**
**disk promoting Elvis's**
**summer festival hung from**
**the ceiling of the Las Vegas**
**Hilton.**
**$85–100**

BELOW: **A full ticket for the**
**Elvis Presley show, held on**
**Saturday, November 24,**
**1956, at the Hobart Arena,**
**Troy, Ohio.**
**$125–175**

pocket calendar; and an 8 x 10-inch color photo of Elvis. The color photograph was the same shot as the bonus photo used for the album "From Elvis in Memphis," except that on the back of the photo was an advertisement announcing Elvis's appearance at the International Hotel. (When it was used as a bonus photo, it included on the back a complete list of Elvis LPs.) To the collector, the most interesting items are the letter from Elvis and the Colonel and, of course, the box.

The 1970 souvenir boxed set was very similar to the previous year's, and it had the same cover with the new date. The box contained: the double record set "From Memphis to Vegas/From Vegas to Memphis;"

a menu, including an introduction by Elvis and the Colonel; a souvenir photo album; a catalog of 1970 records and tapes; the single "Kentucky Rain;" an 8 x 10 inch black and white photo, which was the same as one of the four bonus photos given with the double album "From Memphis to Vegas/From Vegas to Memphis," but with information about the appearance at the International Hotel on the back instead of RCA's list of Elvis tapes; a nine-page press release; and a 1970 pocket calendar.

Although other souvenir packages were given to guests in later years, none of them compares with the 1969 and 1970 boxed sets.

# CHAPTER EIGHT

# THE MARKETING CONTINUES

On the morning of August 16, 1977, as most of the nation that he had entertained and mesmerized was waking up, Elvis was getting ready to go to bed. Some time during that day, he died.

The reaction was immediate and worldwide. Florists throughout Tennesse struggled to meet more than 3,100 requests for floral tributes, and airlines throughout the U.S. filled all their available flights to Memphis as fans began to journey to Graceland. President Jimmy Carter announced that August 17, 1977, would be a national holiday in the singer's honor.

Mick Fleetwood of Fleetwood Mac said that the news "came over like a ton of bricks." Bruce Springsteen said that word of Elvis's death "was like somebody took a piece out of me." Frank Sinatra told an audience in Wisconsin that he had lost a "dear friend" and that the music business had lost a "tremendous asset."

The funeral brought the Mid-South to a halt. Caroline Kennedy covered it for *Rolling Stone*, and among the giants of the entertainment world who attended were Sammy Davis, Jr., Ann-Margret, James Brown, and George Hamilton. More than 80,000 people lined up to pass the open coffin and pay their respects, and a motorcade of fourteen white and cream-colored Cadillacs, with motorcycle outriders, accompanied the hearse on its way to the Presley mausoleum at Forest Hill Cemetery in Memphis.

For many entertainers, death is the end of their careers, but it is a continuing testament to Elvis's title "The King of Rock 'n' Roll" that his popularity continues almost unabated as the twentieth anniversary of his death approaches. Products bearing his name and image are still being produced and marketed, recordings are being reissued and sold as new albums, and movies, TV shows, documentaries, books, and magazine and newspaper articles continue

ABOVE AND RIGHT: **Two of the more popular decanters are the Sgt. Elvis mini-decanter and the large Elvis Teddy Bear decanter. The Sgt. Elvis decanter is a 1984** **Elvis Presley Enterprises product $90–110; the Teddy Bear decanter carries a 1985 EPE copyright $165–250.**

to explore Elvis's life and death.

Just a month after the singer's death, Ronnie McDowell's song "The King is Gone" climbed to 13 in the *Billboard* chart. In 1979 McDowell provided the vocals for the TV movie *Elvis*, and two years later he performed in another TV movie, *Elvis and the Beauty Queen*. McDowell also provided the vocals for the mini-series *Elvis and Me*, which was made in 1988. On February 11, 1979, Kurt Russell portrayed Elvis in the ABC–TV movie *Elvis*, a show that finished with a Nielson rating of 27.3, higher than both *Gone with the Wind* and *One Flew Over the*

ELVIS' TEDDY BEAR
WITH MUSIC BOX THAT PLAYS "(LET ME BE YOUR) TEDDY BEAR"

ELVIS' TEDDY BEAR

McCORMICK DISTILLING CO., WESTON, MO. 64098
80 PROOF • STRAIGHT BOURBON WHISKEY

*Cuckoo's Nest*, which were shown at the same time. Also in 1979, Lena Canada's book, *To Elvis, With Love*, was published. This told the story of a patient with cerebral palsy who had a pen-pal relationship with Elvis, and in 1980 it was turned into a TV movie, *Touched by Love*. On March 1, 1981, NBC–TV screened its own Elvis movie, *Elvis and the Beauty Queen*, featuring Don Johnson, who put on 40 pounds to play Elvis, and Stephanie Zimbalist played Linda Thompson.

By the early 1980s, Graceland had gained a stature that was almost equal to that of the White House. Fans flocked there for anniversaries and memorials. On June 7, 1981, Priscilla Presley opened the mansion to the public, although the upper story, with Elvis's bedroom and private chambers, has never been on public view. The house is a huge tourist draw and is the second most visited house in the U.S. By

1991 it was rumored that the house alone earned more than $50 million annually, and receipts were as much as $20,000 a day from tour tickets alone.

In 1981 the potential of Elvis's posthumous earnings became clear to everyone. Todd Slaughter, a member of Elvis's British fan club, released the album *Inspirations*, which contained previously released gospel songs and which reached No. 5 in the charts. This was followed in October 1982 when RCA released "The Elvis Medley," which included "Suspicious Minds," "Teddy Bear," "Burning Love," "Jailhouse Rock," "Don't Be Cruel," and "Hound Dog."

By 1978 the modern Elvis memorabilia industry had begun to get into gear, and in October of that year *People* magazine noted that a "billion dollar industry" had been spawned when Elvis died, ranging from $1.00 bills (Elvis replaced George Washington) to toilet seats. In August 1984 *Life* magazine was able to comment that Elvis was not only worth more dead than alive, but that his memory was "earning 10 times what he made in his 42 years – and that was $100 million."

In the years immediately following Elvis's death in August 1977, merchandising was uncoordinated and out of control. It was, for example, possible to buy a vial of clear liquid that was marketed as Elvis's sweat, and poorly made products appeared on the scene, to be quickly discounted by fans and collectors alike.

It was not until 1982 that Elvis Presley Enterprises, Inc. gained control over the rights to the singer's name and merchandise, but since then it has been very active in exercising that control. More than 100 companies, large and small, all over the world were granted licences to produce some kind of merchandise, and there have been some lines that have delighted both fans and collectors. Under EPE's control, the creativity and quality of much of the merchandise has been outstanding, and the good-quality memorabilia that is being produced is one of the most rewarding areas for the collector.

For the serious collector, the items from the 1950s will always represent the best. However, the craftsmanship of the modern products makes them worth collecting. Although it is often easy to think only of records, movie posters, and sheet music in any discussion of memorabilia, the scope is far, far wider and even includes Natural Choice Industries' "Love Me Tender" conditioning shampoo, rinse, bath milk, and lotion. All these toiletries were produced in what is now considered to be a very rare carrying case.

ABOVE AND RIGHT:

**Natural Choice Industries introduced a set of hair- and body-care products in a line known as "Love Me Tender." The brand included shampoo, rinse, milk bath, and lotion. An attractive carrying case was available when all four products were bought.**
**Complete package: $100–150**

## PLATES

In a more traditional vein, several companies have produced Elvis plates. Royal Orleans of New Orleans, Louisiana, produced a series depicting Elvis at some of his better known concerts, including "Live in Las Vegas," "Aloha from Hawaii," and the "Mississippi Benefit Concert." The plates originally retailed for approximately $35.

Bill Jacobsen designed a commemorative plate rimmed with 24-carat gold and featuring four versions of Elvis. The plates, manufactured by Nostalgia Collectibles, originally retailed for approximately $45.

In 1977 Limoges of France was commissioned to

RIGHT: **This commemorative plate was manufactured by Nostalgia Collectibles and designed by Bill Jacobson. It was part of a limited edition celebrating the fiftieth anniversary of Elvis's birthday. The plate originally sold for $45.**
$100–150

ABOVE: **This Detroit concert figure was in a limited edition series, produced by Royal Orleans, depicting many of Elvis's most famous concerts. Plates were made to match. The figures originally sold for about $125.**
$125–175

LEFT AND ABOVE: **This brass-plated Christmas tree ornament was introduced by the Hallmark Company** as a collectors' edition ornament. It was copyright 1992 by Elvis Presley Enterprises Inc. $18–22

create an official commemorative plate. It features a portrait of the young Elvis looking off into the far distance. The 7½-inch version originally sold for $25, while the 10-inch plate was priced at $50.

In 1988 the first Delphi collector plate series to feature Elvis was offered through the Bradford Exchange. To date, eight different series, consisting of as many as 16 different plates in a single series, have been created. Each series is based on a theme – Elvis's movies or hit records, for example – and they have become very popular among collectors, with the value of the very first such plate, "Elvis at the Gates of Graceland," issued through the Bradford Exchange, having increased substantially in value since its appearance in 1988.

Other plates that are held in high regard among collectors are those created by the artist Susie Morton

and distributed by R.J. Ernst Enterprises, Inc. The plate entitled "A Commemorative to Elvis" is especially desirable.

## DOLLS

Collectible dolls have ranged from the decidedly shoddy and gaudy to good-quality items that capture and represent the true spirit of Elvis. Soon after his death, a radio in the shape of a doll appeared in Hong Kong. This was tacky and nasty, and was exactly the kind of product that Elvis Presley Enterprises Inc. tried to stop.

To combat this problem, World Doll was licensed to produce the Elvis Presley Limited Doll Series. The five dolls were sculpted by Joyce Christopher. Four of them stand 21 inches high and sold for $100–125.

One of the dolls, a 19-inch "gold and platinum" doll, sold for $285.

In 1984 the Eugene Doll & Novelty Company produced a series of Elvis dolls, and today both the World Doll product and those made by the Eugene Doll & Novelty Company are sought by collectors, which has increased their value.

One line of merchandise that was not only handsomely crafted, but also beautifully packaged, was the series of dolls by Hasboro, marketed under the title "Elvis Presley Commemorative Collection." These were manufactured in 1993 and depict various stages of the singer's career. Although six dolls are known to have been made, only three have, thus far, been marketed.

BELOW: **The vinyl doll, which is 21 inches tall, represents Elvis dressed in a white jump- suit with a flame motif. Part of a limited edition, this is one of the better-made items available to collectors. It was produced by World Doll and designed by Joyce Christopher. $200–250**

CENTER AND BELOW: **This Elvis doll made by Eugene Doll & Novelty Co. (Dolls) stands 12 inches high and carries 1984 Elvis Presley Enterprises copyright. Other Elvis dolls were made by the same company. $75–125**

An associated line of items appeared in 1991, when Hamilton Gifts Ltd., with the authorization of Elvis Presley Enterprises, produced a limited edition of musical figurines and music boxes. Hamilton also offered other Elvis items, including, in 1991, a Christmas ornament, and the following year, Hallmark, best known for its cards and gift-wrap, issued a brass-plated Christmas ornament, retailing at $14.75. Today, the same ornament, which did not sell well in 1992, can be obtained for $18–25.

## CARDS

In 1956 EPE had authorized Topps Gum Company to issue a set of 66 Elvis cards, and the value of these cards has appreciated considerably over the years. In 1978 the license for the cards went to the then fledgling Donruss Company of Memphis, and they produced cards that first sold for fifteen cents a pack. In 1956 each card was hand-colored, but the Donruss set used color only if the original photograph was in color. The value of the Donruss cards has risen comparatively slowly.

In 1992 the River Group Company was authorized by Elvis Presley Enterprises to print three series of cards depicting the singer's life and career. The complete set, entitled "The Elvis Collection," featured 660 cards in both color and black and white, and it included some very spectacular photographs. The set also included a limited number (40 in each series) of "foiled" cards, known as "chase" cards, which carry a high premium among collectors. The whole set is extremely attractive and is certain to rise in value.

In addition to the series of cards in "The Elvis Collection," the River Group Company produced several related items. Customers could, for example, obtain a binder with plastic sleeves in which to store and display their cards, and it was also possible to obtain a large, colorful poster promoting "The Elvis Collection." The same company also produced two other sets – one, of 50 cards, features Elvis's gold and platinum records, while the other, which contains 25 cards, is entitled "Quotable Elvis." There was also a set of 25 color postcards, each 5 x 7 inches.

Items related to "The Elvis Collection," but not available by order from the River Group Company, are the highly collectible life-size standees, which were made specifically for stores to promote the various series. The company also sent out promotional cards to retailers, to introduce and explain the series of cards. Only 10 versions of these "promo" cards were made, and each bears the word "PROMO" in bold type on the back. The most keenly collected of these cards are those in uncut strips of four. Two different strips were produced.

BELOW: **These bubble gum cards were made by the Donruss Company of Memphis, Tennessee. The set is copyright 1978 Boxcar/Factors.**

**Complete set: $40–65**

## CLOCKS AND WATCHES

Perhaps in recognition of the fact that Elvis had a timeless talent, Bradley Time produces a line of clocks and watches, which include a wristwatch, pocket watch, two wall clocks, and a travel alarm. The Pearl Grandfather Clock Company produced a limited edition of the Graceland grandfather clock in 1985. Each of the 6,000 clocks in the edition is hand-carved from oak and features beveled glass and solid brass fixtures.

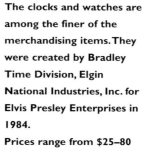

The clocks and watches are among the finer of the merchandising items. They were created by Bradley Time Division, Elgin National Industries, Inc. for Elvis Presley Enterprises in 1984.
Prices range from $25–80

115

## MISCELLANEOUS

In 1984 the Lapin Products Company produced two different toy guitars, each copyright Elvis Presley Enterprises 1984. There was a large black and white, six-string guitar, trimmed with gold and featuring two decals of Elvis from the 1970s on the face. The smaller, four-string version was similar, except the decal on the face was of Elvis from the 1950s. In addition, the background of the packaging of the four-string guitar features three tinted photographs of Elvis from the 1950s.

At the other end of the scale, in 1979 Boxcar Enterprises ordered 100,000 cases of "Always Elvis" Blanc d'Oro wine, which was produced by Frontenac Vineyards of Italy and sold for $4.00 a bottle.

The McCormick Distilling Company produced a series of decanters, the first of which, "Elvis '77," appeared in 1977. This was quickly followed by "Elvis '55" and "Elvis '68." All the decanters were authorized by Boxcar Enterprises, which also licensed another keenly collected decanter, "Aloha Elvis." Since then,

RIGHT:
**In 1979, Boxcar Enterprises introduced "Always Elvis" Blanc d'Oro Wine, which was imported from Italy. Frontenac Vineyards supplied 100,000 cases, and it was originally sold for $4 a bottle. $10–25**

there have been other decanters, including a series that featured Elvis with various pet animals and that had such titles as "Elvis and Hound Dog," "Elvis and Rising Sun," and "Elvis and Teddy Bear." Other popular decanters were "Karate Elvis" and "Sgt. Elvis." McCormick produced smaller versions of its most popular decanters, which they marketed as "mini-decanters."

The McCormick Distilling Company also produced a line of white designer decanters consisting of three different figurines. This may well be the most valuable and attractive of all the decanters that have been produced.

For collectors who are interested in steins, CUI Inc. has issued several different styles, including "The Elvis Postal Stein," which commemorates the famous Elvis postage stamp.

BELOW:
**This porcelain figurine stands 8–10 inches tall and features a 1950s Elvis playing a guitar. It was manufactured by Avon Products and was distributed by Elvis Presley Enterprises in 1987. $50–75**

ABOVE:
**This porcelain figurine, which was manufactured by Nostalgia Collectibles, contains a cassette player with five of Elvis's hits on the player. It is copyright 1985 Elvis Presley Enterprises and RCA. $75–100**

# MODERN MERCHANDISE

The game that allows the legend to live on!

LEFT: **In 1987, Elvis Presley Enterprises produced "Elvis: The Game that Allows the Legend to Live On," which was manufactured by Sulden Inc. $75–125**

RIGHT: **This cassette tape, "Savage Young Elvis!," was never released on an album. It is an RCA Special Products item, which was marketed by Radio Schack. It was released in 1984 by RCA Special Products/ Realistic (M)DPKI-0679. $35–40**

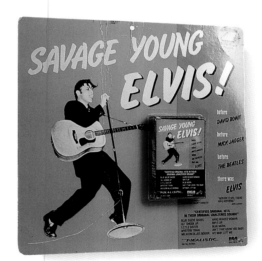

In 1985, Nostalgia Collectibles produced a set of four mugs, 3½ inches tall, trimmed with 24-carat gold. There was also a set of four 6½-inch plates to match. The plates and mugs were named after famous Elvis songs: "Teddy Bear," "Don't Be Cruel," Hound Dog," and "Are You Lonesome Tonight?"
Set of mugs: $30–45
Each plate: $10–20

## POSTAGE STAMPS

It took years of lobbying the U.S. Postal Service (USPS), but Elvis's fans eventually got the USPS to produce an Elvis Presley stamp, and in January 1992 it announced that the singer would be featured on a stamp released on what would have been his 58th birthday, January 8, 1993. The USPS revealed that it would allow Americans to vote on which image they wanted to see on the stamp, and the choices were a 1950s Elvis as a slim, dark-haired boy, leaning forward and singing into a microphone or a heavier, older Elvis, from the 1970s, shown wearing a rhinestone-studded jumpsuit and singing while standing straight up. Artists were selected to create the portraits, and ballot papers were distributed across the country. The USPS organized press conferences, and newspaper articles appeared, arguing the pros and cons of the different images. The USPS even created a set of promotional material to accompany the stamp. Different packages of the stamp could be bought for between $5 and $20, and the entire pack of memorabilia could be purchased for $44. Millions of fans called in and placed their orders.

The stamp depicting the younger Elvis proved to be the most popular.

BELOW: **This is the original 1992 U.S. Post Office poster asking people to choose between the "young" Elvis or the "older" Elvis. Postcards for voting were handed out free to be posted in. Promotional items such as this are difficult to obtain. $50–75**

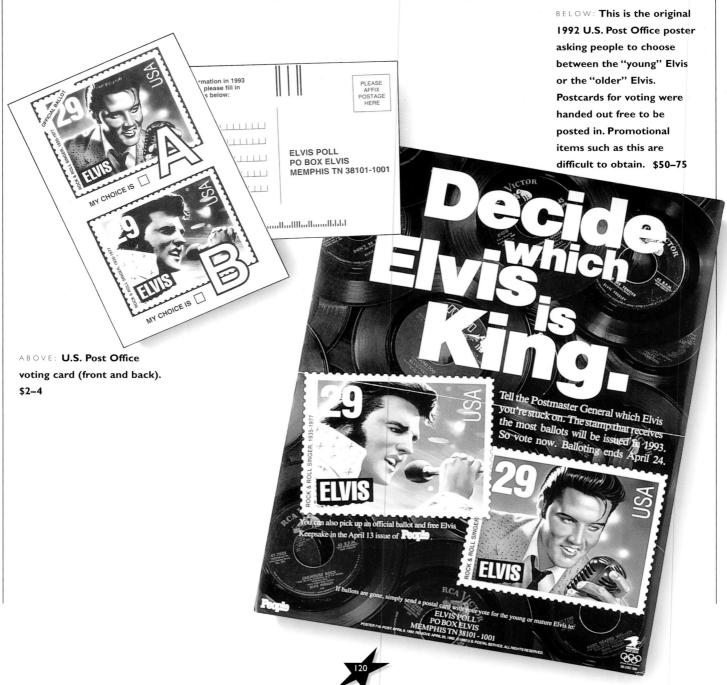

ABOVE: **U.S. Post Office voting card (front and back). $2–4**

When it was time for the USPS to order the stamps, it requested that 1 million be printed, a figure almost double all other first printing and unprecedented in U.S. postal history. By the end of 1993, it had become the most profitable stamp in the history of the U.S. Postal Service. The average stamp will bring in approximately $2 million, while a stamp featuring a celebrity can bring in $5 million. In its

ABOVE: **Bradford Exchange U.S. postage stamp plate, issued in 1993.**
**$40–60**

first year, the Elvis stamp sold between $32 million and $36 million.

In all the hyperbole and anxiety surrounding the issue of the stamp, some confusion was inevitable, creating a collectible for both Elvis fans and philatelists. The postal service mistakenly shipped thousands of the stamps to Amarillo, Texas, 12 days before they were due to be released, and the Amarillo post office sold out its share of the stamps in December 1992, making it an unofficial "first day cover."

## THE LEGEND LIVES ON

If all this seems too much for an entertainer who has been dead for almost two decades, remember that Elvis's popularity continues to grow, far beyond what was intended even by Elvis Presley Enterprises, and years after his death the singer remains a cultural icon, recognizable all over the world.

In 1986, Paul McCartney hosted *The Real Buddy Holly Story*, which was shown on British TV. The show included footage of Elvis in concert at Lubbock, Texas, some time between 1953 and 1955. It is the earliest known footage of Elvis performing. On

LEFT: **The game "Elvis Presley King of Rock" was manufactured by Lee Raymond & Assoc. Co. in 1979. Although it is copyrighted, the game was never licensed. $30–40**

ABOVE: **The "Elvis Welcomes You to His World" game was produced in 1978 by Boxcar Enterprises and manufactured by Duff Sisters Inc. $40–50**

ABOVE: **When it is completed, this 1,000-piece jigsaw puzzle features a beautiful painting of the singer. It was produced in 1985 by Elvis Presley Enterprises. $20–25**

September 22, 1986, the TV series *The Twilight Zone* featured an episode called "The Once and Future King," which told the story of a Presley impersonator who mistakenly killed the real singer.

Elvis's material continues to be used in new works. When the feature film *Lethal Weapon* was released in 1987, Elvis's 1957 recording "I'll Be Home for Christmas" was heard over the closing credits. Tuesday Weld, who starred with Elvis in *Wild in the Country* and who was once linked romantically with the singer, stars in the movie *Heartbreak Hotel*, which was produced by Touchstone Pictures. The film, whose name came from Elvis's first hit single, has Weld running the run-down Flaming Star Hotel. The hotel's name is taken from Elvis's 1960 movie *Flaming Star*, in which Elvis plays a half-breed Native American, forced to choose between his heritages. When his full-bred mother (played by Dolores del Rio) is murdered, Elvis sides with the Native Americans. In the movie *Heartbreak Hotel*, Tuesday Weld is beaten up by her boyfriend. Her son, who is determined to help his mother with her love life and her business, plots to kidnap Elvis and bring him to his mother's hotel.

Hollywood still wasn't finished with Elvis. In 1992, the movie *Honeymoon in Vegas* culminates with a scene in which the star, Nicholas Cage, has to parachute in Las Vegas with a troop of sky divers. These sky divers feature black, combed-back hair; white, rhinestone-studded jumpsuits and gaudy jewelry; and they were called the "Flying Elvis." This movie featured 13 Elvis impersonators and many Elvis hits.

In a completely different field, Russian President Boris Yeltsin revealed on July 8, 1991, that Elvis's recording of "Are You Lonesome Tonight" was one of his favorite songs. Presidential candidate Bill Clinton was honored at a Democratic fund-raising event a year later – the background music was "Don't Be Cruel." On the campaign trail, Clinton napped to Elvis tapes and kept photos of the singer nearby. When he played the saxophone on the Arsenio Hall show, he played "Heartbreak Hotel." That year, both political conventions sported buttons proclaiming "I saw Elvis at the Democratic National Convention" in New York City and "I saw Elvis at the Republican National Convention" in Houston, Texas. Presidents Bush and Clinton are not the only ones to have tried to capture their moment with Elvis. In January 1993, the Richard Nixon Presidential Library in Yorba Linda, California, issued Nixon/Elvis White House wristwatches for $45. The library also offered a large postcard featuring Elvis and Nixon on the occasion of the singer's visit to the Oval Office in 1970.

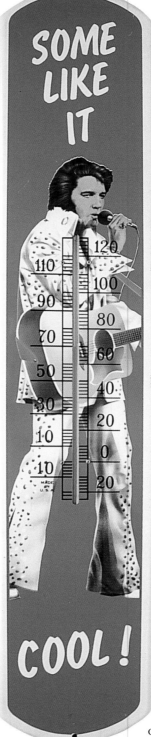

On what would have been Elvis's 60th birthday, *Life* magazine featured a photograph of the singer on the cover. Elvis's name was not shown, and even though it was a decade and a half since his death, there was no need to name him – everyone in American recognized him.

Elvis lives on in other ways. He is the subject of college courses across the U.S. One of the first schools to the study the singer and his influence was the University of Iowa, which offers a course, entitled "Elvis versus Anthology: His Place in World Culture." The Bavarian Motor Works Corporation produced a white BMW 507 called "Der Elvis Wagen"; it retailed at $24,000.

In 1991 Lewis Grizzard noted that CNN had reported that 50 percent of Americans believed that Elvis was still alive. In 1992 CNS news magazine *48 Hours* revealed that 44 percent of Americans were Elvis fans. The Graceland publicity kit boasts that there are more than 450 active Elvis fan clubs throughout the world, more than for any other celebrity.

Even now, Elvis has the largest number of compact disks available of any recording artist, which may seem a little odd when it is remembered that CDs did not exist when Elvis was alive. His songs continued to be heard, and the legend lives on.

ABOVE: **This EPE white metal thermometer sign, which is approximately 40 inches tall, is adorned with a full-length picture of the** **1970s Elvis in white jumpsuit. The sign reads: "Some Like it Cool." $25–40**

## Where to buy

Finding reputable places to buy, sell, or exchange Elvis memorabilia can be difficult, especially for the novice collector. The best place to start, no matter what you are looking for, is, predictably, Graceland. Some other useful addresses are also listed below.

- *Graceland Gifts, 3734 Elvis Presley Blvd., Memphis, Tennessee 38116 (tel: 901-332-3322; toll free 800-238-2000) – offers almost anything you can imagine as long as it is somehow connected to the King of Rock 'n' Roll, including books, compact disks, cassettes and LPs, ceramics and glassware, T-shirts, ties, and even jigsaw puzzles.*

- *From This Old House, P.O. Box 468, Almont, Michigan 48003 (tel: 313-798-3581) – specialty items like wind chimes, T-shirts and nightshirts, books, music boxes, and even a water dome.*

- *Cedco Publishing Co., 2955 Kerne Blvd., San Rafael, California 94901 (toll free 800-227-6162) – stationery and desk accessories.*

- *That'Z Cool Distributors, P.O. Box 14322, Chicago, Illinois 60614-0322 (tel: 312-296-2616) – commemorative postage stamps, puzzles, postcards.*

- *Gifts & Accents, 9611 Metcalf Ave., Overland Park, Kansas 66212 (toll free 800-822-8856) – Christmas ornaments.*

If you want something more personal, D.J. Fontana, Elvis's long-time friend and drummer, will autograph drumsticks. Send a self-addressed, stamped envelope to 4815 Trousdale Drive, #412, Nashville, Tennessee 37220-1324 (no phone calls).

There are a number of documentaries about Elvis, covering everything from his meteoric rise to the top of the charts in 1956 to remembrances of the King and "lost" concert footage, put together in the 1990s:

- *Eddie Brandt's Saturday Matinee, 6310 Colfax Avenue, North Hollywood, California 91606 (tel: 808-506-4242 or 818-506-7722).*

- *Critic's Choice Video, P.O. Box 549, Elk Grove Village, Illinois 60009-0549 (toll free 800-367-7765).*

Advanced collectors might want to approach one of the major auction firms for obscure, specialty, and rare items:

- *Christie's, 219 East 67th Street, New York, New York 10021 (tel: 212-737-6076).*

- *Sotheby's, 1334 York Avenue, New York, New York 10021 (tel: 212-606-7000).*

- *Butterfield & Butterfield, 220 San Bruno Avenue, San Francisco, California 94103 (toll free 800–223–2854)*

Autographs can be acquired from:

- *The Album Hunter, P.O. Box 510, Maple Shade, New Jersey 08052 (tel: 609–482–2273).*

- *Houle Rare Books & Autographs, 7260 Beverly Blvd., Los Angeles, California 90036 (tel: 213-937-0091).*

While Graceland is always a good place to turn to when it comes to starting or expanding a collection, another good resource is a group of people who have been following Elvis for years. The oldest fan club is:

- *The Official Elvis Presley Organization of Great Britain and the Commonwealth, P.O. Box 4, Leicester LE3 5HY, UK.*

To find the nearest fan club to you, call 800-238-200.

Finally, the collector cannot be without the comprehensive guides *Elvis Collectibles* and *The Best of Elvis Collectibles*, published by Overmountain Press, Johnson City, Tennessee 37601 (tel: 615-926-2691).

# THE FILMS OF ELVIS PRESLEY

Listed below are all 33 films that Elvis featured in, followed by the year the film was made, and the actual release date to the general public.

**1.** *Love Me Tender* (1956) 20th Century Fox
Release date: 16 November 1956
**2.** *Loving You* (1957) Paramount
Release date: 9 July 1957
**3.** *Jailhouse Rock* (1957) Metro-Goldwyn-Mayer
Release date: 21 October 1957
**4.** *King Creole* (1958) Paramount
Release date: 4 June 1958
**5.** *G.I. Blues* (1960) Paramount
Release date: 20 October 1960
**6.** *Flaming Star* (1960) 20th Century Fox
Release date: 20 December 1960
**7.** *Wild In The Country* (1960) 20th Century Fox
Release date: 15 June 1961
**8.** *Blue Hawaii* (1961) Paramount
Release date: 14 November 1961
**9.** *Follow That Dream* (1961) United Artists
Release date: 29 March 1962
**10.** *Kid Galahad* (1961) United Artists
Release date: 25 July 1962
**11.** *Girls! Girls! Girls!* (1962) Paramount
Release date: 2 November 1962
**12.** *It Happened at the World's Fair* (1962) Metro-Goldwyn-Mayer
Release date: 3 April 1963
**13.** *Fun In Acapulco* (1963) Paramount
Release date: 2 November 1963
**14.** *Viva Las Vegas* (1963) Metro-Goldwyn-Mayer
Release date: 20 April 1964
**15.** *Kissing Cousins* (1963) Metro-Goldwyn-Mayer
Release date: 6 March 1964

**16.** *Roustabout* (1964) Paramount
Release date: 12 November 1964
**17.** *Girl Happy* (1964) Metro-Goldwyn-Mayer
Release date: 22 January 1965
**18.** *Tickle Me* (1964) Allied Artists Picture Corporation
Release date: 15 June 1965
**19.** *Harum Scarum* (1965)
Release date: 15 December 1965
**20.** *Frankie and Johnny* (1965) United Artists
Release date: 20 July 1966
**21.** *Paradise Hawaiian Style* (1965) Metro-Goldwyn-Mayer
Release date: 8 June 1966
**22.** *Spinout* (1966)
Release date: 14 December 1966
**23.** *Double Trouble* (1966) Metro-Goldwyn-Mayer
Release date: 24 May 1967
**24.** *Easy Come, Easy Go* (1966) Paramount
Release date: 14 June 1967
**25.** *Clambake* (1967) United Artists
Release date: 4 December 1967
**26.** *Speedway* (1967) Metro-Goldwyn-Mayer
Release date: 13 June 1968
**27.** *Stay Away Joe* (1967) Metro-Goldwyn-Mayer
Release date: 14 March 1968
**28.** *Live a Little, Love a Little* (1968) Metro-Goldwyn-Mayer
Release date: 9 October 1968
**29.** *Charro!* (1968) National General Picture Corporation
Release date: 3 September 1969
**30.** *The Trouble with Girls* (And how to get into it) (1968) Metro-Goldwyn-Mayer. Release date: 10 December 1969
**31.** *Change of Habit* (1969) Universal
Release date: 2 January 1970
**32.** *That's the Way It Is* (1970) Metro-Goldwyn-Mayer
Release date: 15 December 1970
**33.** *Elvis On Tour* (1972) Metro-Goldwyn-Mayer
Release date: 6 June 1973

# DISCOGRAPHY

## ELVIS PRESLEY'S TOP TEN SINGLES: DEBUT DATE, TITLE, AND PEAK POSITION

| Date | Title |
|---|---|
| **1956, March 3** | Heartbreak Hotel, No. 1 |
| **May 26** | I Want You, I Need You, I Love You, No. 1 |
| **August 4** | Hound Dog, No. 1 |
| **August 11** | Don't Be Cruel, No. 1 |
| **October 20** | Love Me Tender, No. 1 |
| **November 17** | Love Me, No. 2 |
| **1957, January 26** | Too Much, No 1 |
| **April 6** | All Shook Up, No. 1 |
| **June 24** | Teddy Bear, No. 1 |
| **October 14** | Jailhouse Rock, No. 1 |
| **1958, January 27** | Don't, No. 1 |
| **January 27** | I Beg Of You, No. 8 |
| **April 21** | Wear My Ring Around Your Neck, No. 2 |
| **June 30** | Hard Headed Woman, No. 1 |
| **November 3** | I Got Stung, No. 8 |
| **November 10** | One Night, No. 4 |
| **1959, March 20** | I Need Your Love Tonight, No. 4 |
| **March 30** | A Fool Such As I, No. 2 |
| **July 6** | A Big Hun O' Love, No. 1 |
| **1960, April 4** | Stuck On You, No. 1 |
| **July 18** | It's Now Or Never, No. 1 |
| **November 14** | Are You Lonesome Tonight?, No. 1 |
| **1961, February 20** | Surrender, No. 1 |
| **May 15** | I Feel So Bad, No. 5 |
| **August 21** | Little Sister, No. 5 |
| **August 28** | His Latest Flame, No. 4 |
| **December 4** | Can't Help Falling In Love, No. 2 |
| **1962, March 17** | Good Luck Charm, No. 1 |
| **August 4** | She's Not You, No. 5 |
| **October 20** | Return To Sender, No. 2 |
| **1963, June 29** | Devil In Disguise, No. 3 |
| **October 19** | Bossa Nova Baby, No. 6 |
| **1965, April 24** | Crying In The Chapel, No. 3 |
| **1969, May 3** | In The Ghetto, No. 3 |
| **September 13** | Suspicious Minds, No. 1 |
| **November 29** | Don't Cry Daddy, No. 6 |
| **1970, May 16** | The Wonder Of You, No. 9 |
| **1972, August 19** | Burning Love, No. 2 |

## ELVIS PRESLEY'S TOP TEN ALBUMS: DEBUT DATE, TITLE, AND PEAK POSITION

| Date | Title |
|---|---|
| **1956, March 31** | Elvis Presley, No. 1 |
| **November 10** | Elvis, No. 1 |
| **1957, July 22** | Loving You, No. 1 |
| **December 2** | Elvis' Christmas Album, No. 1 |
| **1958, April 21** | Elvis Golden Records, No. 3 |
| **September 15** | King Creole, No. 2 |
| **1960, May 9** | Elvis Is Back, No. 2 |
| **October 31** | GI Blues, No. 1 |
| **1961, July 10** | Something For Everybody, No. 1 |
| **October 23** | Blue Hawaii, No. 1 |
| **1962, July 14** | Pot Luck, No. 4 |
| **December 8** | Girls! Girls! Girls, No. 3 |
| **1963, April 20** | It Happened At The World's Fair, No. 4 |
| **September 14** | Elvis Golden Records Vol. 3, No. 3 |
| **December 21** | Fun In Acapulco, No. 5 |
| **1964, April 11** | Kissin' Cousins, No. 6 |
| **November 14** | Roustabout, No. 1 |
| **1965, April 17** | Girl Happy, No. 8 |
| **August 14** | Elvis For Everyone, No. 10 |
| **November 13** | Harum Scarum, No. 8 |
| **1968, December 21** | Elvis, NBC-TV Special, No. 8 |
| **1973, February 24** | Aloha From Hawaii Via Satellite, No. 1 |
| **1977, July 23** | Moody Blue, No. 3 |
| **October 29** | Elvis In Concert, No. 5 |

ELVIS PRESLEY

Vocal accompaniment:
J.D. Sumner & The Stamps

MONO
74-0769